Regulating in The Public Interest:

Looking To The Future

Edited By
Dan Corry

CONTENTS

page

PREFACE

Regulation is one of the key instruments of modern micro-economic management. Some see it as an alternative to ownership. More accurately one should recognise that ownership is simply one possible way of regulating.

This set of essays represents a forward look at what may happen in the utilities, so giving a context in which policy choices can be made both in terms of what we want to achieve in these areas and how regulation might be organised to help achieve them.

The key point that needs to be recognised is that the future is not pre-determined. In some sectors, like telecoms, technology and international forces are certainly driving the agenda and making the policy options seem constrained. But even here the regulatory structure and the policy it is asked to implement can have profound implications for what the future looks like. Equally, as the industry evolves, both policy and regulation will need to change to reflect the new reality. In sectors such as rail, gas and electricity, the future is even more up for grabs.

It is because we do have power to influence the way these key industries and their associated services develop that the issues must be considered seriously. We therefore present an analytic introductory essay that tries to give some guidance as to why we are regulating and what the ideal system needs to be able to cope with.

The individual views expressed on the specific utilities in the rest of the papers are the authors' own. All of these papers were prepared for a conference organised by IPPR and sponsored by Unison. However the papers do not necessarily reflect the views of either IPPR or Unison. We present them as stimulating and positive forward-looking contributions to this important debate.

Dan Corry
May 1995

WHY SHOULD WE REGULATE -
AND WHY IS IT SO COMPLICATED?
DAN CORRY[1]

The regulation of our great utilities is in a mess. Recent events have put the spotlight on decisions made by un-elected and unaccountable regulators, making policy decisions apparently on the hoof with no sense of stability at all. In such ways they determine the future shape of major sectors of the UK economy without any clear driving force in terms of democratically determined decision-making. Often they make pricing and other changes that seem biased to one set of interests rather than another, yet with little rationale or explanation given.

Most would agree that this state of affairs cannot continue into the second half of the 1990s whichever Party is in power. The task therefore is to look ahead and to consider how the regulatory structure and system can be amended.

Of course from a free market perspective, most of the problems outlined above stem inherently from the misguided attempt to regulate rather than try and abolish regulation.[2] Such a viewpoint would have us push ahead on injecting more and more competition into the regime so that the regulators can be put out to grass. Then, they would say, all would be simple.

In the real world however regulation of most of the utilities will continue to exist and will be complex. It is vital to establish clearly why this is so, so that any re-ordering of the system takes full account of these issues.

Where we are

Only 16 years ago all the utilities were in the public sector and they were run in accordance with the wishes of the government of the day. There were some rules and guidelines within which the nationalised industry bosses had to operate, and frequently there was direct interference in day to day issues by ministers. Ownership can in this sense be seen as a particular form of regulation.

The Conservatives were not prepared to give up regulation when they undertook the major drive to privatisation (motivated to a large extent by the desire to raise money). Indeed, since in most cases they initially just created private monopolies it is hard to see that they could have avoided it altogether. But rather than spell too much out (or think things through), the government simply appointed a single person to regulate each of the new sectors with very vague terms of reference that usually consisted of looking after the consumer, making the firm viable and promoting competition. In practice almost all regulators have taken the opportunity to push as hard as they can along the competition road, mimicking it where they could not deliver it. In telecoms, new technology has destroyed many of the monopoly problems and made this a realistic aim. In water, where competition makes little sense, the regional monopolies have been maintained and little real competition seems likely. Gas and electricity find themselves between the two extremes: network monopolies appear here to stay, but much competition has been brought into supply in the larger, business market and the aim is to bring competition into the domestic market.

On the whole, though, developments in each sector have been driven by the aims of the regulators, their own preferences and inclinations and the relationships they have with their industries. It is this fact that needs to be questioned.

Why Regulate?

For those who see competition as the answer to everything, regulation is simply an orderly way of moving from a one-firm industry to a free market. But for the left, the aims are broader.

In the first place we should be clear that we regulate not because of any desire for control or power - a sort of poor man's nationalisation - but because we believe that it can help achieve public policy objectives more easily than can other measures.

Outside the utilities, regulation is often a response to information asymmetries (hence restrictions on the behaviour of insurance companies, health and safety legislation and so on) or due to externalities (control of unsafe industrial practices for instance). In the utilities, issues of natural monopoly, inherent in networks, and social policy objectives are often as important.

Yet while this gives a fairly clear rationale for regulation it does not tell us much about how to regulate. It could be that regulation is fairly simple - name your objective and the tools and structure fall into place. But our contention is that the regulation of the utilities is and will always be a complex task.

The reasons for this reflect three distinct issues. First, the economics of the situation are not at all straightforward. Second, it is highly likely that the public policy objectives will go beyond the pursuance of competition or the control of monopoly and it is almost certain that this set of objectives will not be mutually consistent. Third, there is a perceived need to try and secure the advantages of arms-length regulation of the utilities at the same time as guaranteeing that such regulation is accountable to the democratic process.

The Simple Economics of Regulation?

Monopoly Regulation

In a simple textbook world, the regulation of a private sector monopoly appears to be fairly straightforward. Left alone, the monopoly would restrict output and raise prices. The regulator therefore places restrictions upon its behaviour. In the UK case these restrictions have taken the form of ceilings on the price that can be charged to consumers (by defining the maximum annual price increase allowed as being 'X' percent less (or more, in the case of water) than inflation - as measured by the retail price index or RPI). The monopolist is then free to maximise profits and it is assumed that they do this by minimising costs. In such a way the best outcome will be produced.

In practice the fact that the regulator does not have anything like perfect information on crucial aspects of what they need to set 'X' - things like the cost structure of the monopolist - makes life more complicated, so that the appropriate restrictions are not always clear. Risks of regulatory capture or deceit by the monopoly need to be faced up to and as recent events in the electricity area show, it seems that the regulators will often only have the information that the regulated monopolies want them to have.

On the technical side, one can argue the pros and cons of rate of return (or profit) caps relative to price caps. Some recent thinking argues that pure price cap (RPI-X) regulation raises the cost of capital.[3] It certainly gives rise at times to levels of profits that the public finds hard to stomach. One idea that has been floated in an earlier IPPR publication[4] is to link the X factor to the profits or dividend payout of the regulated firm. This might give the firm itself an incentive to balance properly the interests of shareholders and consumers without the need for constant regulatory interference. Such an idea might be particularly applicable in the water area where the existence of regional monopoly firms is likely to last for a long time, if not forever.

We conclude therefore that even in the supposed simple case of the regulation of monopolies, regulation, if by no means impossible, turns out to be far from straightforward.

Regulating Structure

However severe complications enter the picture the minute that the regulator wants to try and alter the structure of the industry. In particular the regulator might believe that, or be instructed by legislation to act on the assumption that, only the injection of more competition into the industry can really secure the best deal for consumers and the nation alike. Moving from a monopoly industry to a competitive one must involve the encouragement of new entry and from this stem a whole host of difficulties that may exceed anyone's abilities.

In the first place we should note the fact that encouraging duplicate services where we are talking about networks or major installations or investments, will be costly. While the extra choice will undoubtedly be welcome, encouragement of such activity will not invariably produce the best outcome for the consumer let alone maximise society's welfare function - which includes other things as well.

But let us say that we do want to encourage at least a degree more competition. Encouraging entry can take several forms.

First, the regulator discriminates in some way in favour of the entrant. If a new entrant will need to build up infrastructure that would not be viable without protection then this may be inevitable. But how much protection? How do we make sure that it does not last for ever through 'new entrant capture'? Dare a regulator let an encouraged-in entrant fail?

Alternatively newcomers can be absolved from some of the regulation imposed on the original monopoly, particularly things like the obligation to serve all customers at reasonable prices. But as debates around gas illustrate this is as likely to lead to market segmentation, as new entrants cherry-pick, offering lower prices to well-heeled customers, as it is to competition.

It is clear then that making judgments in the name of pursuing competition will be difficult in many areas. The decision of how far to go, what pace to move at, when to stop, are not clear ones that a computer or technical manual can give definitive answers to.[5] At the very least they need a clear assessment of the costs and benefits of different approaches. Faith is not enough.

Second, the regulator may feel that the utility is irredeemably characterised by natural monopoly in at least some of its aspects, so that encouraging more competition in here is not worthwhile. However this need not prevent them from believing that some functions of the 'monopoly' are contestable and they may therefore want to force competition into these areas, effectively de-integrating or breaking up the business. Hence the transport of gas or electricity (a natural monopoly) is split off from its ordering, metering and invoicing to customers.[6]

However the drive to introduce competition wherever possible has fallen foul of a lacuna in economic theory. In truth we do not know what the appropriate or optimal boundary of a firm should be. Where is the boundary where organisation gives way to the market? We certainly know that if we had to recontract for our jobs every day, recontract the rent and so on there would be masses more competition but we would be so busy recontracting we would get nothing else done! Clearly there is something about transactions costs that must be at the bottom of this[7].

Businesses are generally integrated to the extent they are, because the transaction costs are too great in introducing yet more market relations and because such relations mean that spill-overs, synergies and so on are no longer kept within the profit centre. It is not at all clear that firms in competitive markets contract out anything and everything that cannot be tied exactly to their supposed 'core' business. Therefore we cannot be sure that this is the correct strategy to impose on the regulated utility sector.

It appears that in general, regulator-induced divestment of a function by a regulated company leads to a sharp increase in paper-work, policing and transaction costs in general (just as the health reforms, by introducing market relations, have vastly increased the number of administrators). Interestingly some believe that if takeovers within (and between) utility sectors are allowed, the private sector will bring about the re-integration of these industries.

Now none of this is to say that the benefits from the competition introduced in this way cannot outweigh the costs outlined above, but it does make clear that at the very minimum it is unacceptable to simply act with a blind faith in competition. Some sort of assessment of costs and benefits must be undertaken.

The third form of entry comes through the fact that privatisation has opened up the utilities to the market for corporate control, i.e. the threat of takeover. Such a market is held to be crucial in keeping managers on their toes. But the threat has to be carried out at least occasionally in order to be real and effective. Yet do we want electricity regions merging? What are the implications of letting French water companies take over British ones? Is it a good decision for the consumer - or indeed competition in the long run - if a major international conglomerate takes over a UK electricity company? In the water area, where in trying to produce pseudo-competitive outcomes, the regulator can only judge things via so-called 'yardstick' competition, there may be problems if the potential number of comparisons are reduced[8].

We see then that the competition issue does not give an easy mapping to action. This not only tells us that regulation will be complex and decisions often debatable but should make us concerned that regulators today are operating in such a very broad framework that they can simply act upon their own prejudices without having to argue that hard for them. They do not have to defend themselves or pay any explicit attention to estimates of either the overall costs and benefits of an action or the distribution of these costs and benefits.

The Case of the Conflicting Objectives

The other set of problems for regulation of the utilities stem from public policy objectives. This may have no connection to the monopoly issue although the two are often inter-connected.[9]

Such public policy concerns fall into two main types:

First, the service concerned may be considered such a staple of life and vital ingredient of citizenship as to be what is often called a 'merit' good. This is a service that society decides should be provided on similar terms to all consumers irrespective of the differential cost of provision to different types of consumer.

Moreover, if a consumer cannot pay, something other than the normal commercial response of withdrawal (i.e. cut-off) is generally expected. And the quality of the service may also be a matter of public concern with society unwilling to allow people to choose 'poor' water for a lower price even if it were technically feasible. Of course this means that regulation will have to go beyond price or profit.

In all these cases it is clear that the issue turns on political decisions as to what constitutes equitable and reasonable treatment rather than being primarily a matter of regulatory discretion.

Second, the government may have strategic interests specific to that industry in question. For example in the case of energy, it may wish to achieve a certain degree of diversity of source. Or it may have environmental objectives which - for some reason - it cannot pursue with differential taxes.

In these cases government should set out its policy and embody them in the set of parameters within which the regulator or regulators must work.

In theory it is clear that utility regulation should be used as a tool to achieve public policy objectives only where the public policy issue at stake is specific to the industry in question. More general divergences between private and social cost and benefit that happen to occur in a particular regulated industry but are also found elsewhere should be dealt with by general measures.

For instance, there is a strong case for saying that if unemployment is an issue then government should act generally to put it right rather than act to make specific industries, that happen to be regulated for reasons other than labour market ones, behave differently. Similarly, if the use of excessive energy leads to detrimental environmental effects then the energy price should be altered so affecting all industries in a similar way rather than introducing incentives to energy efficiency via the regulation of the gas and electricity sectors. And if one is really worried about the poor's lack of access to the vital utilities of life one should simply give them more money, by redistributing through the tax and benefit system, not demand all sorts of cross-subsidies from richer to poorer consumers within the regulated utilities.

However, this is in many ways a counsel of perfection. In practice we are in second best worlds where for a variety of reasons we have not set prices (like energy) correctly, where government has leverage - through regulation - over things like the pace of adjustment in some industries but not in others, and where attempts to deal with issues like equity directly through the tax and social security system are likely to lead to a whole host of economic distortions in themselves so that they are not a 'pure', non-distortionary alternative.[10] In such a world judgment will be constantly needed.

Competition and Public Policy Objectives

To the extent that public policy objectives can be achieved through competition these issues become less important. But how far can this take us?

Equity considerations have generally been accepted as being beyond markets. However, Stephen Littlechild, the electricity regulator, recently argued that "in a fully competitive market all customers are potentially attractive to suppliers". Of course, in one sense this must be right for at some price and under some conditions the market will always deliver. But just as those who sell bread in the local shop to those who cannot drive to the supermarket, charge higher prices (so that the poor generally pay more for their food) so the electricity company will want to make sure that serving the poorer customer does not reduce their profitability. Pre-payment meters, seen by the advocates of competition as the way that the market will solve the 'poor' consumer problem, are in fact just a way of the firm getting money up front and shifting all the risk onto the consumer - who in practice self-disconnects when times are hard. The equity problem can hardly be said to have been solved in this way.

Another argument that profit-maximising, private utility firms will continue to serve the less valuable, less well-off in a purely competitive market bases its case on consumer morality. The head of Consumer affairs at OFGAS recently claimed that the universal service obligation will continue to be met not because of action by the regulator but "because market forces demand the services are provided". He explained, "If any company fails to meet the needs of all strata of society in its chosen supply area, word will soon get round and that company will be blacklisted - so much so that customers will exercise their freedom to choose and go to another supplier".[11] Maybe, but there is little evidence that when John Lewis closed down their stores in less affluent areas of London, any better off customers boycotted their Oxford Street stores. But maybe it will be different with gas!

It seems therefore that whatever the benefits of competition it will not deliver in this area and there is an overwhelming case for regulation to achieve equity goals. This makes the 'political' nature of what we want the regulator to do quite apparent. We can deliver the equity goal through obligations on the incumbent, or cross-subsidy, or industry levies, but deliver it we must.

Another key public policy objective, with particular applicability to gas and electricity, is the need to increase energy efficiency and so reduce energy use. The government has recently claimed that this environmental objective can be achieved through competition alone. Rejecting a levy on gas bills to fund energy efficiency measures, the government has argued that competition itself will lever in benefits as firms grow up offering packages that include energy efficiency as a means of winning more business. Whether this is likely to work to any great extent, particularly when the environmental problem is fundamentally about externalities that no consumer will take into account in their behaviour, is highly questionable.[12]

Multiple and sometimes conflicting objectives therefore do seem to be a real issue and cannot be magically waved away by the introduction of competition. Judgements will have to be made, trade-offs determined and balances struck. The question is who should make them?

How do we Build a Dynamic Regulatory Structure?

The third major reason why regulation will always be complex is institutional. The arguments above compellingly show that regulation is not merely technical. For this reason there is a strong presumption in favour of the process being open, challengeable in some way, and ultimately, in one form or another, accountable to elected people. On the other hand, one of the great advantages of the privatisation process has been to remove from politicians the temptation to intervene regularly, but unpredictably and inappropriately, in the day-to-day decisions of the utilities.[13]

This is an issue that goes way beyond the regulation of the utilities, particularly as the fashion in public sector management has gone decisively in favour of agencies, quangos, independent central banks and other bodies over the last few years. On the whole everybody would agree that elected people should set the policy and that the agency (regulator in our case) should simply implement it. But this leaves open the degree of discretion that the regulator will have to carry this out.

Some have argued that we can do no better than the current system. John Kay for instance, believes that imperfect though it is, if we reduce the discretion of the regulators we can only effectively give back the detailed decision making to the politicians, which is worse, or on to the judiciary, which could be the worst of all worlds.[14]

It is strange however, that the theoretical reasoning that says that politicians cannot be allowed to be too involved because they will begin to pursue their own objectives and not those in the best interest of the nation (a theory incidentally that should never have led to privatisation in the first place[15]), is not applied to the regulators themselves. Regulators who are more or less unaccountable will undoubtedly follow their own agenda unless their discretion is limited (a point forcibly argued by Peter Spring in this volume).

Another approach, again accepting the basic desirability of 'agencies' with a great deal of discretion, is to seek to keep the independence of the regulatory quango but in some way make it itself contestable and open to 'takeover'.[16] However both of these positions seem to take a very pessimistic view of our ability to marry the democratic process with arms length approaches to policy implementation.

If we are clear about the differences between policy and structure then perhaps this need not be so much of a problem. Surely the democratic system is capable of deciding that it wants for instance to have equal prices for everyone for domestic gas, or that it wants a 10 per cent reduction in total energy use per household over 10 years, or that it wants no more than say 40 per cent of the energy market to be provided by one energy source. It can then tell the regulator to deliver. This does not remove all discretion from the regulator but circumscribes it. The alternative is such a broad remit - as at present - that the regulator cannot be stopped from anything much.

Such an approach is more akin to that put forward by Dieter Helm. He believes that the government should set out its broad strategies for each sector, and produce a White paper setting out the broad methodological approach to be used for the calculation of things like cost of capital, asset valuation, price setting and so on[17]. Such an approach could also include targets and performance indicators to give the public some power of scrutiny over the actions of the regulators who are, after all, acting on their behalf.

In addition, if there is to be discretion it certainly seems unwise to leave it to one single individual and therefore the commission approach argued for previously by IPPR,[18] where the 'head' regulator is the first among equals rather than the lone decision maker, must be a part of any new regulatory settlement.

There are many more suggestions around as to how to make regulators accountable and yet free from too much interference. The balance will always be difficult to get right but that is no excuse for not trying.

Implications

Several vital conclusions come out of the analysis above which should influence any progressive reform of the regulation of the utilities in the future.

First, to re-amplify the conclusion of an earlier IPPR study (*Regulating our Utilities*), the pursuit of competition cannot be the only objective and nor - to the extent that it is an important policy aim - is it unproblematic. Regulation involves judgements about the distribution of costs and benefits which are for politicians and not technocrats to make. These decisions must therefore be made in an accountable framework and the current system is not acceptable.

Second, where regulation is being pursued to bring about a change of structure (usually to increase 'competition') it should be preceded by a careful study and cost-benefit type analysis. It is very important that regulators should account for the probable costs as well as the putative benefits of introducing competition. And because these are judgments the whole system must be open and challengeable in some way.

Third, it is legitimate and sensible to have public policy objectives in many of these areas although the costs and benefits of different ways of achieving them must always be borne in mind. The focus should be on the best way of using the system to deliver them and not on the red herrings of whether competition will deliver them all on its own or arguing that they are always and inevitably a problem for some other branch of policy.

Fourth, it is clear that regulation is no substitute for policy. The answer to "what do you want to do with the energy sector" cannot simply be "regulate it"! This opt out of policy making must be exposed wherever it exists.

Some argue further that policy must logically come prior to regulation and that discussions of regulation are in some sense putting the cart before the horse. Now it is certainly true that regulators can only act to deliver a policy when they know what it is. But we do not need to wait upon precise policies before trying to determine appropriate structures for regulation. The analysis presented here suggests that we must have more accountability and openness and the structure we build must take account of this. Ideally it should also be able to cope smoothly with changes of policy. The exact structure of regulation may be 'informed' by the specific policy but the whole shape should be independent of it.

However, if we do produce a better split between policy making and the carrying out of it, the failure to make policy will become more exposed and politicians will find it harder to hide behind regulation.

Time to Act

The argument that the current structure of regulation is fine is one that is hard to accept. This is based not so much on a critique of the actual way the process has worked to date nor of unhappiness with some of the decisions that have been made, but from our understanding of the reasons for regulation and the role it should play as an agency for implementing policy. For these reasons, the problems are not solved if one simply replaced current incumbents with what Dieter Helm calls the 'right chaps' to, for instance, be tougher on prices.

Regulation is not just the new way of government control of industry, now that public ownership is unfashionable, but reflects the new agenda of setting frameworks in which the private sector can flourish to the benefit of us all. For this reason getting the institutions right matters enormously.

Notes

1. Dan Corry is the Senior Economist for IPPR and editor of the quarterly journal *New Economy*. He co-authored IPPR's publication *Regulating Our Utilities*. He would like to thank Gerry Holtham for several of the ideas in this paper and Randi Hawkins, Dinah Roake, Stephen Tindale, Phil Burns and Spencer Livermore for helpful comments on the text.

2. Not all on the right believe this. Cento Veljanovski argues that "The issue is not one of voluntary run-down of regulatory activity, but of planning for permanent regulation" (in *But who will regulate the regulators?* Adam Smith Institute 1993).

3. Colin Mayer: 'Why are utilities so risky?', *Utility Finance*, January 1995, OXERA.

4. 'The Future for Utility Regulation: Economic Aspects' by Mike Waterson in *Regulating our Utilities*, by Corry, Souter and Waterson, IPPR 1994.

5. An example of the contested terrain of competition and the interests of the consumer comes from the telecoms sector where recently some have argued that the price cap on BT is so severe it is hampering new entry to the industry with detrimental effects on consumers ('Telecoms regulation 'stifles competition' *Financial Times*, 15.3.95). Similarly, OFGAS has argued that the use of highly publicised minimum service standards by British Gas is in fact anti-competitive and so against the consumer interest.

6. When the network is to be left as a monopoly but competition is to be enhanced by allowing different companies to have access to use the network, the regulator then has to work out fair and efficient terms for that access, which is another huge area of 'technical' debate.

7.   See Gerald Holtham and John Kay, 'The Assessment: institutions of policy' in *Oxford Review of Economic Policy*, Autumn 1994 for discussion of some of these issues.

8.   Asked about a proposed water merger, a spokesperson for OFWAT said a merger "could impact on [the regulators] ability to carry out his statutory duties because it would reduce the number of comparators that would enable him to make comparisons about efficiency, etcetera and to set the relevant price-limits" (*Guardian,* 7 March 1995).

9.   There may be good reasons to regulate for the public good even where the industry is not characterised by monopoly. In banking for instance there are restrictions on banks to ensure solvency. Equally some argue that policy should ensure that everyone has access to a bank account and credit card. However in practice, if we are not regulating an industry directly because of 'economic' factors, we are more likely to use other methods to ensure things like universal access.

10.   Andrew Dilnot of the Institute of Fiscal Studies has forcibly argued against using regulation to deliver equity goals ('What role for the State in the Economy' ESRC/RSA seminar, 1994). However this is a simple extension of the purist economists case for level playing fields in the first best world and fails to relate instruments and outcomes to social welfare functions or indeed the real world.

11.   Willie Macleod: 'USOs and the Restructured Gas Industry' - paper give at Centre for the Study of Regulated Industries seminar, 29.3.95. Of course his argument assumes that it is possible to create genuine competition in the domestic gas market in the first place.

12.   See *Guardian* 9.3.95 for the Government line and Gill Owen 'Energy Services Market: Will Competition be left to chance' (Energy Saving Trust and Gas Consumers Council, 1994) for some doubts on the idea. Regulation could of course help - for

instance a minimum allowed price (as well as a maximum) so that competition would be as much about efficiency as about price.

13. This is in many ways a 'side-benefit' of privatisation. Much of it was inspired by the desire to reduce the public sector and get round Treasury rules on public expenditure rather than to solve the government failure problem. How big this latter problem was in reality is not something we debate here.

14. John Kay, 'The Regulation of Monopolies' in *But who will regulate the regulators, op cit.*

15. See Sam Peltzman: 'The economic theory of regulation after a decade of deregulation', *Brookings Papers on Economic Activity*, 1989.

16. See for instance Mulgan in *Oxford Review of Economic Policy* Autumn 1994.

17. See for instance his comments in 'The Regulatory State', *Analysis*, BBC Radio 4, 20.10.94.

18. See David Souter: 'A stakeholder approach to regulation' in *Regulating our Utilities, op cit.* Many other proposals for reform are put forward in this publication but are not repeated here.

MUDDY WATERS:
THE FUTURE FOR WATER SUPPLY AND SEWERAGE
DAVID KINNERSLEY[1]

An Industry Exposed

The label 'privatisation' can refer to all sorts of formats for combining necessary public provision with some participation by private business. Some of them hardly require access to significant private capital, and do not involve asset-sales or changes of ownership.

The barriers coming down are in large part the demarcations that it suited Westminster and Whitehall to keep so rigid: the genuinely mixed economy can move forward to a new stage of maturity. But some new identities and new relationships in the minds of customers need to be established with respect to the utilities, especially for services on which the whole public depends but which are also monopolies in private hands.

In 1995, five years or more on from the flotation of gas, water and electricity, this does not seem to be going well. Even the government seems unsure enough of public attitudes to the idea of having essential services in private hands that they are holding back from clearly intended further privatisation - such as the Post Office.

The water supply and sewerage companies seem to be a special case. They have the least prospect of competition, with no substitutes for delivery and collection of a product used in so many ways. They have the lowest of reputations now with the public.

Indeed, they are a special case in at least two other ways. First, it was generally agreed that they had to achieve an investment approaching £500 per head over ten years for the whole population of England and Wales for a largely static volume of demand. This was partly to catch up on the spending on renewing the infrastructure that the government had held back on in the public sector through much of the 1980s; and partly to secure cleaner rivers and beaches and better drinking water, a real and necessary upgrade for a crowded island. Second, the water industry was also the one utility which was private already in the supply sector for about a fifth of the people, mainly in towns. For a century or more, these companies, owned and financed by private investors, had kept such a low profile co-existing with the town hall operations of water supply and sewerage, and later the larger regional units, that at privatisation in 1989 their odd predicament of suddenly being given a new regulator was hardly noticed.

Now the industry seems to have gone from the shortcomings that go with having too little to spend on renewals and upgrading to a flamboyance associated with companies that have more money than they know how to spend wisely - or forgo in lower charges. For an industry traditionally committed to calm and vigilant routines in providing for uses that are mainly a matter of unthinking habit, this is a dismal change: the genuinely mixed economy is proving less ready to adapt and find new types of company style than might have been hoped. At present the water companies appear exposed, even vulnerable, to hazards that are mostly of their own making and caused by energies misdirected and by inertia.

This paper is concerned with the present state of affairs in 1995 so as to locate some foundations for looking into the future. Can we foresee remedies to be put in place for present discontents, or further hazards that will have to be addressed? To steer through the confusion that may be shown to be prevailing among the leadership of the companies as well as the public, we focus on three main issues:

- performance and profitability;
- activities outside the core business;
- charging policy and debt.

At this stage, not too far from an election, the broad questions have to include not only what the industry may do for itself, but also what this or that government might do to it, possibly through new powers or guidance for the regulators. But first, we need to outline how the two types of companies came to their present frameworks.

Privatisation

For the different types 'companies' involved, water privatisation was really a very different process and experience, and broadly, those concerned in each group have reacted somewhat differently since.

The ten regional water authorities (in England and Wales but not Scotland) lost their river functions but gained their freedom from a Whitehall control that had become a repressive centralised harness once the majority representation of local elected councils on their governing boards was ended in 1983. At least as significantly, they also negotiated write-offs of all National Loans Fund debts of some £5 billion, a net cash injection of £1.5 billion to their several balance sheets, and provision for a capital tax allowances of £7.7 billion. A green dowry, as it was called, for a divorce sounds odd, but very generous it was: they were being divorced, as it were, from the public sector as a seeming liability.[2]

The flotation of this most unpopular and uncertain of privatisation was nearly six times subscribed, with a share premium to the end of the year (taking account of other market movements) of more than 11 per cent over the offer price. The changed prospect, added to the largesse of the green dowry already mentioned, was steadily rising prices through the Retail Price Index + K price cap formula (for early years with K factors set by Ministers, later on by OFWAT). This was to be in return for carrying through investment programmes which would cost upwards of £24 billion at 1989 prices.

On the other hand were the 30 or so water supply only companies, long private, which had survived with little change the 1974 regionalisation. In 1989, little change was perhaps a harsher fate: no write-offs of debt or cash injections from the public purse to their balance sheets, which continued much the same. The main new feature for them was to be the new regulatory regime under OFWAT (which they would share with the ten water and sewerage PLCs - WSPLCs - with unchanged boundaries), in place of the simpler limitation on dividends and profits they had before.

Recently, some of the WSPLCs (Thames and North-West especially) have attracted much censure for extravagant rewards to their top executives (as indeed have gas and electricity companies). Some have tried to brazen this out with references to their wide-ranging adventures overseas.

But confusion prevails among the companies. Amid this flamboyant posturing as serious entrepreneurs with customers to keep satisfying, all the companies have joined together to press Ministers to allow them to continue some mixture of old-style town hall rates and new-style council taxes as the main method of charging domestic premises for water services. One of the first legislative moves in the road to privatisation was made in 1988 by Mrs Thatcher's government. This was that the rates method must end by the year 2000. Yet by the end of 1994, the companies had moved barely 10 per cent of some 18 million households to other bases for charging, though charging by volume of service taken (ie through meters, as in other utilities) had been made widespread for business premises. Using old town-hall methods to get much of their income, in advance and with a sequence of increases above inflation, hardly fits with the water companies' would-be image of global entrepreneurs.

But it is worth repeating that there are more modestly conducted companies, though they can hardly avoid the poor public reputation which the others establish in the public mind.

Excess Profits?

In actual service-delivery, there is probably little to choose between most of the companies in each of the two groups. The customers may be more aware of water supply - since it comes towards them - than of sewerage, which is a carrying-away service. In their areas, most of the water only companies also collect the charges for the sewerage companies, so they must keep in line on this.

Most people spend little time reflecting on where their waste water goes, but thanks to the environmental lobbies and the well-regarded

National Rivers Authority (NRA), the fact that water supply and sewage disposal both widely use much the same river capacity is better understood. There is wide support for safeguarding cleanliness and improving standards both of rivers and of beaches. In general, the companies in both services can probably claim that technically they are reliable enough, and that the fact that they are local monopolies does not cause problems for their customers.

However, it is disturbing that a Consumers Association report (Which, September 1994) gave the lowest mark for customer satisfaction among five utilities to water companies (30 percent, against an average of 40 percent among four others). The total of complaints reaching OFWAT in 1993, at almost 55,000, is about the same for the electricity regulator, and notably less than for the older Gas Consumer Council.

The CA research found that 23 per cent of water users thought that the service was poor or very poor value for money in terms of the services and the charges levied (where the figures for other regulated services were BT 16, Electricity 13, Gas 9, and Post Office 5). This could simply reflect difficult public adaptation to a harsh global trend: water is widely getting more costly to supply and treat because of increased demand and spreading pollution. But it suggests at least some discomfort with the incidence of current charging methods.

But another outside comparison is available from an article recently published in Paris.[3] This shows that, in terms of operating profit as a proportion of turnover, a level of 9-12 percent for one of the large French companies (Lyonnaise des Eaux) from 1976-1984 has been squeezed down to less than 7 percent during the period 1984-1992. By contrast, three years of a similar calculation for the ten British WSPLCs show figures consistently of 30-36 percent, with Thames and Northumbrian somewhat lower in the 20-28 percent range, and Welsh up at 47-51 percent. On this comparison, the British level of profits seems to be, as a regular thing, about five times the level taken by French companies in the same situation.

The French companies do not own the assets long-term, so they do not have to earn so much in return upon them, but they do finance much renewal, and have to recover the cost of doing that. The French have nothing of the same centralised regulation that OFWAT provides, but rely on the companies desire to retain and regain municipally-organised franchises and the necessary goodwill for that. The feeling of competition is more effective in the minds of the managers, because the municipality can at intervals decide not to renew the franchise of the present company.

Finally, there is OFWAT's own thoroughly prepared assessment of the profitability of the core services. Since 1991, profits before tax have increased in real terms by 21 per cent. In current cost terms, they amounted in 1993-94 to £1.41 billion (after a £60 million restructuring provision by Anglian). That is almost as much (in one year) as the government's cash injection at the time of flotation. The percentage of current cost profits retained in the business had been 41 percent in 1992-1993, but fell slightly to 38 percent the next year. These latter figures give some indication of the extent to which customers may be said to be directly financing new investment for the future from the level of current charges they are paying: the companies might have borrowed more, and taken less from customers, as in many other industries. Capital investment in 1993-1994 was £1.6 billion on water and £1.3 billion on sewage. These figures show that upwards of 60 percent of profits are going elsewhere.

The return on capital in 1993-94, based on the current cost operating profit and the regulatory capital value developed during the Periodic Review, was no less than 12.1 per cent, and was remarkably consistent on the same basis for the previous four years, being in the range 12.1 -12.8 per cent. In the next ten years, for which OFWAT has set limits on K factors and charges in the Periodic Review, it has felt able to do so on the basis that returns would fall to about half this level in real terms over 10 years. Looking at the CA figures for customers' view of value for money, and the very different levels of profitability prevailing in French water supply, it seems necessary to ask: why spread the achievement of that reduction over as long as ten years? At the end of this period, the figure will still be a reasonable return on capital in this low-risk business. Small wonder that customers may feel, so to speak, 'ripped off'. No wonder that recently North West Water has announced a rebate for customers as well as a bonus for shareholders. It almost shines like a good deed in a naughty setting. Will others follow?

Diversification Problems

Non-core activities of the water companies are not affected by regulation save for OFWAT's commendable struggles to maintain transparency and prevent cross-subsidisation. The core business nevertheless provides a very stable background for them.

The ten WSPLCs have been more adventurous - and imprudent - in diversification: the water only companies generally cautious. Is this the effect of longer experience in the private sector or of no green dowry? The adventurers, however, have been nothing like so well rewarded as in their home monopolies. Thames and North West have lost upwards of £40 million between them according to the most recent figures published. None of the WSPLCs has made 20 per cent of turnover as operating profit, and only three companies (Yorkshire, Southern and Wessex) have achieved or bettered 10 per cent.

Much of the diversification within the UK has gone into businesses which can benefit from the huge investment programmes being undertaken in core services. Independent plant manufacturers and consulting engineers have been taken over by the companies and organised in new groupings, for overseas as well as UK marketing. But because of its capital intensity, ability to win much business overseas, either for design or for operating packages, is much influenced by the financial manipulations involved rather than the relevance and efficiency of the packages offered. Several Australian states, for example, are being pursued with blandishments from NorthWest and other companies when they are perfectly able to get design or operating arrangements within Australia: privatisation, as they embrace, it may be mainly a new way of borrowing external capital.

Meanwhile, many of the nations that really need expatriate operating skills and capital urgently are those least able to afford the cost and offer any margin of profit. There will be a strong trend of population moving to urban centres, but much of it will be to informal settlements, not calm leafy suburbs. Big money for water supply and sanitation may depend greatly on international banks and aid programmes.

As John Kay has pointed out recently[4] there is little or no direct benefit to British water users in diversification overseas, and not much indirect benefit either so far. The posture of facing global competition may even be, paradoxically, self-indulgent as much as would-be heroic.

The Case for Meters

Despite their desired dynamic, global image, it is interesting to note that the main contact the water companies have with every customer at home, is slipping a bill through the letter box and insisting on payment in advance: the companies cling strongly to the old Town Hall method of charge for most households. To whatever degree the public could be led into accepting it, the companies do not want to promote metering despite it being the usual means of charging for other utility services. It would bring, of course, payment largely in arrear of usage, uncomfortable for their cash-flow. It would bring probably a lot more queries (they would actually have to speak to more customers, and visit them to read meters: arbitrary demands by post and threats to disconnect are much less hassle). It shows signs from trials of somewhat reducing consumption, so the bills of many households might go down possibly more than the rest would go up. Moreover, OFWAT has studied it thoroughly and done their best to press down on the transfer fees and standing charges that companies have loaded on to the minority who enquire about making the change.

One regional company says almost with pride that only one in three of those who ask for details go ahead. Is that discouragement what the company intended?

Labour understandably worries about metering for two main reasons: low-income households generally facing bills that will be less predictable under metering, even if they are lower, and households with high water usage for large families and invalids. In part, these worries may take too little account of another problem - at least one person in five living alone and paying the same old water bill based on the rateable value of the property over 20 years ago, with a hugely increased regional poundage. If the companies were ever to be allowed to use the council tax as the basis for charging, would they apply the rebates and exemptions that council tax includes - or confuse the public with claims that it is only the property bands on which they want a cheap and convenient piggy-back? It should be out of the question that they are ever granted the choice of using old rateable value or the new council tax band, whichever suits themselves best. The changes of incidence in moving to council tax may be as much bother as significant moves to metering would bring, and still not achieve a basis of charge seen as fair in other utilities.

Moreover, with metering, there could be an imaginative diversity of tariffs. The companies have to reduce their return on capital under the OFWAT price-caps: there may be money there to help with hard cases and present areas of overcharge; the Income Support provision for water bills could also be made more refined at probably little extra total cost. The transition from rateable value-based bills to usage-related ones could be greatly eased by keeping down standing charges and spreading the change over three or five years (less rateable value, more metered component in each year).

This would require time, of course, and more attention and effort by the companies. A recent study of debt and disconnection in water bills shows some companies have been much less flexible and helpful (in providing for more frequent 'easy' payments) than others.[5] The fact that these difficulties - almost two million households defaulted on their water bills during 1994 - occur under the present system of charging mostly from old rateable value hardly sounds like a convincing argument for keeping it going, or giving the companies carte-blanche to find other methods. One way forward might be for the companies to use, with suitable customer liaison and information, much more metering while getting guidance from local councils about properties or families that might be more fairly charged on a council tax basis for water. Blocks of flats and multi-occupied buildings also need special tariffs as generally their plumbing systems cannot be segregated. The most important point is that the customers should feel they have influence over the way their consumption gets reflected in their bills.

The water companies have let their inertia get the better of them in this crucial and practical problem after a dozen or so small trials of metering in various localities. It hardly seems a credit to the power of privatisation to promote innovation.

Perhaps unsurprisingly, the Government has recently (April 1995) announced that they will continue on with the rateable value approach, thus turning away from the Thatcher viewpoint. Though not ideal, this is probably better than moving to the council tax approach or indeed of giving companies a choice between the council tax and the rateable value base for charging. The Government also appears to be committed to encouraging the further use of metering. One might expect that over time metering will increase and the situation will then be reviewed. Use of massively out of date rateable values is surely not a tenable long term solution.

New Styles for Water Companies

This paper started from arguing the need to form a new style - for essential public services now in private hands. That is a challenge in part to what companies make of their relation with the regulator. It does not follow that if they satisfy or obey him in the narrow range of matters where he has notable power, they may do as they wish elsewhere, in core or non-core services. They still have a public whose regard they surely need to gain and retain, for the sake of commercial and political security.

This applies to charging methods in particular. It applies also to takeovers and mergers, which are still subject to approval even when golden shares are ended. Interestingly, the first bid for a regional company may be from a French group already established in water-only companies in its region.

It would be good for the processes of interchange of experience to see how the French might manage one of the regional companies: their record in water-only companies does seem to carry seed of a more enlightened approach, and in France they have much longer experience of conducting themselves as private operators of essential services, in the energy field for example and in undertaking as well as in water.

This raises again the question of whether the core services benefit or suffer from the adventures in non-core services, where so far they lose money or bring only small profits. This is the one direction where the regulator might be given an additional duty - not so much to judge the merits of non-core ventures (Heaven forbid) but to require divestment of all non-core businesses if it appears that, because of those distractions, the group seems to be giving less than full-hearted and sensitive attention to the changing set of problems arising in its core business. Perhaps even the granting of such power to a regulator would have a sobering effect on the companies without his having to exercise it much.

In general, though, more powers for the regulators does not seem the way forward, even though on executive pay or other matters, Tory or Labour parties may see it as relevant to public misgivings without bringing too many problems back to the desks of Ministers.

The real need, if public misgivings are to be diminished, is for the companies themselves to find that new settled and sensitive style which has eluded them so much of the time since flotation. Their leading executives include those with years of experience in the public sector and those with none. Between them, can they not find a style which recognises that the public sees them still as monopolies, but with a new freedom that they have to use in new ways that fit with the monopoly role rather than appearing to represent a cavalier abuse of it?

Labour would clearly have a good case for insisting on the return of the cash injections in the green dowry to the Treasury: but might be most unwise to think of buying the industry back while it is in such a profitable but problematic muddle. If prices are to be reduced, and given charging will continue not to be based on metering, the vital thing would seem to be to have some regard to local operating costs, in each district, and to squeeze down charges where present distortions most overload them in relation to costs. The standing charges on metered accounts need also to be driven down as far as possible as OFWAT has been trying to do. The folklore that almost all the industry's costs are fixed costs has never seemed convincing despite the capital intensity of the business.

For the Conservatives, the good news is that one of the aims of water privatisation, namely to get access to significant private capital for a huge investment programme, has succeeded. But the bad news is that in so many other respects, especially in charges, the result has been such that 'disappointing' is an understatement.

Whitehall can no longer be blamed as it could in the 1980s. The result so far is of little credit to the idea that privatisation fosters innovation. Perhaps the water industry, as the record of the old private companies confirm, was always wedded to routine. It has now been placed in a far more exposed position. Sadly it shows few signs of yet working out how to handle that.

Notes

1. David Kinnersley held various posts in the water industry in the 20 years up to 1983. Since then, he has been at different times a Fellow of Nuffield College Oxford, a freelance adviser internationally on water institutions, and a member of the National Rivers Authority for its launch and first two years. He is an additional member of the Monopolies and Mergers Commission for water references.

2. National Audit Office report on the sale, HMSO Feb 1992.

3. *Annales des Mines*, end 1994.

4. *Daily Telegraph* (20.3.95).

5. *Water Debt and Disconnection*, Herbert and Kempson, PSI, March 1995.

REGULATING TELECOMMUNICATIONS
DAVID SOUTER[1]

Telecommunications was the first British utility to be privatised and regulated by a non-ministerial department. That department, OFTEL, provided a model for the regulation of other utilities. But the industry OFTEL regulates has been transformed beyond recognition since its establishment eleven years ago. The relevance of its remit and methods of working have increasingly come into question.

This paper suggests how the regulation of telecommunications should change to meet the demands of an industry now radically different from that privatised in 1984. It is in three sections:

● the first describes the transformation of the telecommunications industry over the last decade and the context in which regulation must work;

● the second sets out the current regulatory framework and assesses its relevance to today's and tomorrow's telecommunications industry;

● the third puts forward recommendations for reform, focusing first on competition policy, and secondly on public service needs.

The paper argues that telecommunications regulation today is trapped by the industry's history and thereby failing to address the real issues posed by its present and future. Like other regulators', OFTEL's remit needs to be adjusted to address a wider range of policy requirements and make it more accountable to the public interest. But more than others', its remit and methods of working need fundamental revision if it is to move from yesterday's challenge - of liberalising an entrenched monopoly - to ensuring that a newly competitive market functions fairly and effectively and continues to meet public service needs.

The Telecommunications Industry

Telecommunications is different from other utilities - and is becoming more so day by day. The differences are important to understanding how and why the industry should be regulated.

Firstly, and most importantly, there is the pace of technological change. Telecommunications technology is changing more rapidly than almost any other in human history. The computing power at the heart of telecoms networks and the transmission capacity of radio and fibre optic cable are multiplying almost exponentially. The services and service standards they can deliver to both businesses and residential customers are improving dramatically year by year, and even month by month. No other utility is experiencing this pace of change, nor is any likely to do so.

Secondly, through a combination of liberalisation and new technology, telecommunications has become far more competitive than other utilities like gas, electricity and water:

● BT's monopoly over customer premises equipment was broken many years ago, and it now holds a small fraction of the customer hardware market.

● Its dominance of international and long-distance telephony has been cut to just over 70 per cent and 80 per cent respectively, and is falling in each case by about 4 per cent a year.

● Its share of residential customers, while still around 97 per cent, is being eroded by cable companies holding local franchises for both telephony and broadcast transmission. These are taking 50,000 customers a month from BT and (according to OFTEL) could take as many as 100,000 a month - the equivalent of 4 per cent a year - by the end of 1995.

● Mobile telecommunications is beginning to be extensively used as an alternative - or complement - to voice telephony.

● Niche markets in data transmission and value added services are well-developed, with BT playing an important but by no means dominant role.

There are now significant parts of the telecommunications industry - customer equipment, some niche services, even one important geographical area (the City of London) - in which BT is a minority rather than a dominant competitor. Over 150 firms hold licences to provide telecommunications services, and there is a presumption in favour of granting new licences unless there are substantial grounds against. Competition, in other words, is well established and becoming more extensive at an accelerating pace.

Thirdly, if the nature of the telecommunications industry differs significantly from other utilities, so does its 'social architecture' - because, for the customer, telephony is about networking rather than networks.

● Telecommunications is a largely interactive process, in which the network transmits information *between* customers rather than delivering a product like water or fuel *from* supplier *to* customer.

● Telecommunications is not directly essential to life in the same way as water, light and heating. One can live without a telephone, but cannot fully function as a citizen - and it is this which gives telecommunications the same utility status which has been traditionally accorded to the postal service.

Fourthly, telecommunications differs from other utilities because increased usage is of benefit rather than social disutility. Increased use of water and energy has substantial social costs because of increased pollution and the depletion of finite natural resources. Increased use of telecommunications has no such costs: indeed, it can reduce pollution and energy use by substituting for other human activities (such as commuting) and by making information and services more accessible.

These differences suggest that telecommunications should be regulated differently from other utilities. There should, for example, be less need for intervention to foster competition, as competition is already extensive and increasing. There should be more need for flexibility to deal with rapid changes in technology and in the structure of the industry that it entails.

Regulation needs to reflect these differences and adapt to changing circumstances. This capacity to adapt is even more needful because of three further changes taking place in the telecommunications industry: its globalisation, its convergence with other data transmission industries, and the movement towards an 'information society'. The plot runs more or less like this:

● In the early 1980s, telecommunications was predominantly concerned with what the industry calls POTS - the 'plain old telephone service' based on voice telephony, a service largely undifferentiated between customers except in the volume of connection time, and delivered in each country by national, publicly-owned monopolies.

● Today, business and residential markets are much more differentiated, thanks to the development of data and value added services; and today's multinational businesses are increasingly demanding seamless global service from telecommunications businesses that are competing internationally for their lucrative custom.

● Tomorrow's communications industry will be dominated by a vast range of new services - what the industry calls PANS (or 'pretty amazing new stuff') - provided globally by competing multinational, multimedia businesses, and locally by thousands of niche companies operating across the boundaries that have divided traditional communications industries. POTS could make up as little as 30 per cent of telecommunications business in the European Union by the end of the next decade.

Three processes are involved here:

Firstly, the major telecommunications companies - including BT and some of its UK competitors (AT&T, the US companies that own most of the cable industry, and - to a lesser extent - Cable & Wireless) - are transforming themselves into global communications companies, offering a multiplicity of rapidly evolving high-technology solutions to very large business customers, often through a bewildering web of international alliances. However dominant the domestic market remains in current company cashflow, it is the contest to serve lucrative international business customers and high-volume users that is the key to company survival and success, and that therefore dominates corporate decision-making.

Secondly, telecommunications is converging rapidly with other industries that transmit information, such as broadcasting, computing and publishing. In the past, these relied on different technologies. Now they increasingly use a single method of transmission, doing their business by sending bits of digital data between computers over networks that act as if they were computers.

The capacity of future broadband networks to transmit such data will exceed any feasible level of demand, while the technology itself makes no distinction between the kinds of information transmitted over it - between voice telephony and broadcast entertainment, videoconferencing and data communications between mainframe computers. As transmission technologies converge, telecommunications and broadcast transmission companies alike wish to make full use of their networks to transmit these indistinguishable bits of data, and it is only rational that the quasi-infinite capacity of their networks should be used to do so. This lies at the heart of BT's desire, in the UK, and its American competitors' in their US territories, to be allowed to deliver broadcast entertainment over their telecommunications lines.

Which brings us, thirdly, to the much-hyped 'information superhighway'. There is enormous potential in the new technology to provide new services - commercial and non-commercial, to business and residential customers, for schools and hospitals, across international frontiers and within village communities. The nature and scope of these services is almost impossible to predict - as, at this stage, is their level of take-up in the residential market. Both potential and take-up can be stimulated or constrained as a result of regulation. However, the opportunity of new technology will almost certainly lead to far greater diversity of service provision, with two main consequences:

● New lines of difference in business function will be drawn within the communications industry, between (for example) the generation of content, packaging of information, network transmission and the provision of access for subscribers. These distinctions will replace those between today's telecommunications, broadcasting and publishing industries as the key lines of demarcation within communications. Some businesses will be active in more than one of these areas; others will remain niche players.

● The diversity of services used by different customers will continue to grow. The kinds of service used by multinational business are already hugely different from the basic voice telephony service which dominates the residential market. Small and medium sized businesses, too, make use of a far wider range of services than they used, many tailored specifically to meet their needs. This process of diversification between customers is facilitated by differences in access modes - for example, between conventional and ISDN lines - and will continue even if residential customers begin extensively to use new 'superhighway' services.

The nature of the changes taking place in the communications industry will be revolutionary in *impact* but evolutionary in *process*. There will be no 'big bang', but a rapid, month by month, incremental change in the nature of services provided and the ways in which they are used.

Today's telecommunications industry is therefore utterly different from that privatised - and brought under regulation - in the early 1980s. Tomorrow's will be more different still. The pace of change is so fast that telecommunications companies are forced to revise their corporate strategies every two or three years. How far has OFTEL kept up to speed?

Telecommunications Regulation Today

The present structure of regulation in telecoms looks as follows. Telecoms licences are awarded by the Department of Trade and Industry, but it is OFTEL - the Office of Telecommunications - that has responsibility for managing those licences in pursuit of objectives set out in the Telecommunications Act, as interpreted by its Director-General. Some aspects of the industry are regulated by separate agencies, including the Independent Television Commission (cable company franchises) and ICSTIS (premium service content).

According to the Telecommunications Act, OFTEL should, *inter alia*:

● promote competition in telecommunications services;

● ensure provision of specific public services, including an emergency service, public call boxes, directory enquiries and services in rural areas;

● promote the interests of consumers - specifically including pensioners and those with disabilities - in terms of price, quality and variety of service;

● ensure that licensed telecommunications operators are financially viable;

● promote research and development in telecommunications;

● and contribute to the international competitiveness of the domestic telecommunications industry.

Its prime responsibility, however, according to successive Directors-General, has been the promotion of competition - initially through a duopoly designed to allow Mercury to establish itself as a competitor for mainstream telecommunications services; more recently by facilitating the entry of new competitors into the market, including that of cable television franchise-holders into local telephony. The present Director-General, Don Cruickshank, describes his mission as being to achieve markets with at least three competitors throughout the telecoms sector, including local infrastructure - though in some geographical areas and niche markets this must be impossible to achieve.

Regulation of BT is extensive, and has become more so over time. The main regulatory instruments deployed by OFTEL include the following:

- the imposition of a price cap on a basket of BT services equivalent to about 60 per cent of its turnover, currently RPI-7.5 per cent. This effectively sets a price ceiling for other operators, who seek to undercut BT's tariffs by a margin of about 10 per cent;

- subsidiary price caps on individual tariffs within the overall basket (RPI±0 per cent), on access (rental and connection charges, RPI+2 per cent) and on connection (£99+VAT);

- universal service obligations on BT (in most of the UK) and Kingston Communications (in the City of Hull), requiring them to provide telephone service at a geographically averaged price to all who reasonably require it, along with public services including the emergency service, a directory enquiry service (which may be charged for) and payphones in uneconomic rural locations. BT is also required to provide a Low User line rental rebate and a relay service for the hearing-impaired;

- regulatory oversight (and in effect determination) of interconnection charges between BT's network and those of other operators, including - in theory - the payment of access deficit contributions, to cover the loss BT makes on providing access to its customers to other operators. These contributions have to date been almost entirely waived as an instrument of market entry assistance;

- constraints on BT's ability to offer tariff discounts, and a requirement not to price services below fully allocated costs without the regulator's express consent;

- the introduction of accounting separation, to prevent cross-subsidy between the 'network' and 'retail' elements of BT's business, accompanied by the disclosure of information on BT's internal accounting to facilitate investment decisions by market entrants;

- constraints on BT's involvement in the supply of customer apparatus, requiring it to move towards a rate of return on that business closely equivalent to that made on its core telecommunications services;

- a restriction on BT and Mercury, known as the 'asymmetry rule', which prevents them delivering broadcast transmission simultaneously to more than one household over their main telecommunications lines - *i.e.* to combine the transmission of telephony and broadcasting, something which is uniquely permitted to cable television companies in order to facilitate their market entry into local telephony.

This regulatory framework has three characteristics which set it firmly in the past rather than the future.

- It operates almost entirely by regulating BT rather than the market as a whole.

- It regulates basic telephony services rather than the wider range of services now offered, particularly to business customers.

- It regulates a domestic telecommunications market rather than placing it in the context of developing global competition.

All of this made sense in the early 1980s. Then, the government's objective was to break BT's stranglehold on the telephony market, and a regulatory régime designed to attack BT's entrenched position was the obvious way to do so. However, that is no longer the major issue. What matters in telecommunications competition today is not how fast the provision of basic voice telephony can be diversified, but how competitive will be the additional service offerings that accompany it and are becoming central to tomorrow's communications culture. It is competition in the new marketplace that should interest OFTEL now, not competition in the old.[2]

And herein lies its problem. While telecommunications companies revise their strategies repeatedly in the light of changing market circumstances and technological innovation, their regulator's remit has changed hardly at all. A regulatory régime designed to break a national monopoly has survived almost intact into an age of global competition. It has already outlived one generation of telecoms technology; it cannot possibly meet the demands of another.

OFTEL has begun to acknowledge these changing circumstances - putting forward proposals for moving towards a more open regulatory régime, and preparing to consult on multimedia services. This development is both necessary and welcome, but the regulator's prime focus still remains on the problems of the past - BT and telephony - rather than the competitive, multifaceted 'bit transmission' industry of the future.

Elsewhere[3] I have argued that regulation should serve two main purposes:

● It should balance the interests of the various stakeholders who have an interest in the performance of a utility and the service it provides - particularly those of different categories of consumer.

● And it should promote other public policy objectives determined by government, including (for example) the provision of universal service, the efficient use of natural resources and the competitiveness of UK industry.

This balance of objectives is particularly hard to achieve in telecommunications, where new technology has displaced an historic homogeneity of service offerings. It is necessary, nonetheless.

In the past, business and residential customers - the highly profitable and the marginally 'economic' - both principally used a single service, basic voice telephony. The provision of universal service (the key public service element of telecommunications) required little more than balancing the costs to different groups of consumers for this largely homogeneous service.

Today, there is a fundamental division between the dynamic, highly competitive, international market for business communications - centred around new services undesired or unavailable in the domestic market - and the public utility service required by residential customers, which is largely based on voice telephony. These divergent product ranges are still naturally provided by the same companies, but while managers concentrate on the burgeoning profitability of international business communications, public policy remains focused on equitable provision of relatively unprofitable basic services in the domestic, national market.

Regulation is further complicated by the crucial role which communications industries will play in economic development over the next decade. Countries which have dynamic resident telecommunications players stand to gain substantially from their international competitiveness, through the export earnings and inward investment that they stimulate and attract. Their governments have an interest, therefore, in ensuring that they succeed in international markets as well as contributing to public services at home.

Telecommunications regulation has sought - with increasing difficulty - to serve two purposes: to facilitate the development of a competitive market and to maintain the provision of public service. The time has come to distinguish more clearly between these objectives, and find new ways of satisfying public service obligations within a competitive framework.

In the remainder of this paper, I make some proposals about how this might be done. My aim is to identify a regulatory framework that is appropriate for the future - flexible enough to adapt to the twists and turns of an industry in continual change; to meet public policy objectives including the modernisation of infrastructure and the competitiveness of Britain's communications businesses; and to fulfil the basic utility (or public service) requirements for which this profitable, competitive, international industry remains responsible.

Recommendations for Change

Communications is likely to prove the transforming instrument of a new industrial revolution over the next generation - the printing press, the railway of its day. Any government that fails to develop a vision - as the US government has done through Vice-President Gore's National Information Infrastructure initiative - of what this technological revolution can mean for its economy and society is failing in its responsibility to its citizens.

It is the job of an elected government to establish this vision and the policy framework needed to achieve it, not that of an appointed regulator. Regulators should be civil servants, accountable to government and Parliament: they should implement policy, and not determine it.

As we have seen, the present regulatory framework for telecommunications is deficient for its purpose. However relevant it may have been in 1984, it has failed to keep pace with the rapidly changing communications industry. It must be transformed to meet tomorrow's needs, on which it must now focus.

I have suggested that there should be much clearer distinction between the regulation of competition in telecommunications, and regulation to secure public service objectives. The two need to coexist within a single regulatory framework, but that should recognise the increased diversity of services and markets which telecommunications operators serve. This section focuses first on the regulation of competition, and then turns to regulation for public service.

Regulating the Market

Radical changes are needed to bring the regulation of telecommunications into line with today's communications industry.

First, the regulation of transmission - which is primarily economic in purpose - should be separated wholly from regulation of content - which is essentially social or political. There are many important issues in content regulation - including diversity of ownership, the security and privacy of information, copyright and access to pornography. Different technologies and methods of transmission pose different problems of enforcement, but no differences of principle. They should be dealt with accordingly.

Second, the regulatory structure must adapt to match the industrial structure that it regulates and needs to regulate in future. Telecommunications and broadcast transmission use the same technology to do the same thing - to move bits of data from one place to another. Their infrastructures compete with and complement one another. To regulate them separately leads to inconsistency and incoherence. All regulatory functions concerning the digital transmission of information - whether in OFTEL, the ITC or elsewhere - should be brought together in a single regulatory authority for communications.

It follows, third, that all competing networks that transmit bits of data should be allowed to do so regardless of their content. Artificially segregating 'telecommunications' and 'entertainment' transmission no longer makes any technical or economic sense.

The 'asymmetry rule' barring BT and Mercury from combining telephony and broadcast transmission should be lifted, over a period, in line with the recommendations made by the Parliamentary Select Committee on Trade & Industry. Asymmetry has helped to foster competition for local voice telephony, but is now deterring infrastructure modernisation by BT and Mercury and encouraging lower-quality infrastructure investment by cable companies. It tackles yesterday's problems, but is storing up greater ones for the future, and will lead to less competition in tomorrow's services and less choice for tomorrow's customers. The franchise-by-franchise lifting of asymmetry recommended by the Select Committee would allow gradual transition towards a market based on the realities of digital data transmission, without disrupting the development of competition in local telephony.

Fourth, and in line with this, the regulatory authority should recognise new lines of demarcation within the communications industry - where the crucial distinctions lie between network and service provision, not between telecommunications and broadcasting (or, for that matter, between fixed network and mobile technologies). It would be a mistake, however, to confine individual firms to specific parts of this new industry. That would second-guess its likely development - something no-one should be rash enough to try.

The key issue is that of access to networks. The regulator should ensure that every service provider can make its services available to every customer over every network - and that no network provider seeks to restrict routes to market for its competitors. (Providers of computer operating software may pose as great a threat as network operators in this respect.)

Fifth, the regulator should recognise that competition is already extensive in much of the communications market, and will continue to develop rapidly in those areas of geography or service provision where there is sufficient customer demand to offer competing operators an adequate return. This is particularly so in high-volume business markets and in the value-added services which will provide the bulk of telecommunications business by the end of next decade.

The regulatory framework should look ahead to a time when the market is fully competitive, rather than harking back to the days of BT's monopoly - it should focus on competition, rather than competitors. In this scenario:

- Regulation would focus on the market as a whole and not on a single player. The rules that apply to one company would apply to all. Market entry assistance would be phased out, and a level playing field established between all operators, subject to the rules of normal competition law.

- Interconnection prices would become a matter of negotiation between operators, subject to general competition law, rather than being determined by OFTEL.

- The constraints imposed on any operator's tariffs would be lifted, again subject to the general provisions of competition law against predatory pricing.

- Most important of all, the overall price cap on BT's services would be replaced by competitive tariff-setting, with specific price caps retained only where needed to address problems of market failure or of equity towards specific groups of potentially disadvantaged customers.

Of course, a transition from regulated liberalisation to the application of general competition law could not take place overnight. The constraints imposed on BT would need to be relaxed gradually. But the assumption of any future regulatory framework should be that it is to regulate a competitive industry and not to constrain a former monopolist - and to do so by intervening where necessary rather than where possible.

Sixth, the regulatory framework should recognise the international context in which today's telecommunications companies compete. Domestic markets may provide their critical mass, but it is international business that provides their dynamic growth and the basis for their success or failure. Britain offers a degree of market entry assistance to its own telecommunications companies' competitors which is unparalleled in other countries, including the United States where many of those competitors are based.

Ownership does matter in this context. The export revenue and contracts for suppliers generated by a successful resident communications company are of considerable benefit to the country as a whole. The regulator should pay attention to the overall impact of his decisions on the competitiveness of telecommunications businesses in the international markets that matter most to their commercial futures. This includes reciprocity of market access.

Market entry assistance also needs reconsideration. Short-term assistance for new entrants may be needed to stimulate competition, but its retention for longer than necessary to do this will lead to misplaced investment decisions and the development of new vested interests intent on maintaining the market distortions that assistance inevitably creates.

Market entry assistance for major *multinational* telecommunications companies is no more necessary in Britain than in other European countries whose markets they are preparing to enter following liberalisation later this decade: it should be removed.

Lastly, the regulatory framework should reconcile the need for flexibility - to respond to the rapid and continuing changes in communications technology and international competition - and that for stability - to give businesses the chance to plan ahead with confidence.

The capital costs and time required for major network modernisations in communications infrastructure are very large - perhaps £15 billion and 15 years in the case of BT's domestic network. But the evolution of technology and service provision is much more rapid than this. Even for very large, profitable companies like AT&T and BT, the risks associated with major investments are very high - and the only certainty is that the risk of not making them is higher still.

These risks are not just confined to the communications companies themselves. Thousands of firms in Britain depend, to a significant degree on supplying communications equipment. Their competitiveness, too, depends on being able to plan ahead - knowing they will have a market for their products, and that it will not be jeopardised by outmoded regulatory constraints.

The need for flexibility, meanwhile, means that the regulator may need to use class licences and codes of practice much more in future, rather than direct intervention, to regulate both telecommunications operators and service providers. Otherwise, the administrative burden of the process may prove unnecessarily bureaucratic and inefficient

Regulating for Public Service

These changes reflect the need for the regulation of competition to adapt to the technological transformation and global competitiveness which characterise today's telecommunications industry. But telecommunications is not just a business like any other. It also provides a public service, and it has become accepted as an essential good - something almost everyone thinks is necessary to function effectively within society. However small a proportion of telecommunications business voice telephony becomes in future, and however little it contributes to the profitability of competitive global companies, it will remain the essential service for residential customers because it provides access to emergency services, information, and the opportunity to participate fully in society.

At privatisation, ministers argued that competition would benefit all customers and did little or nothing to address their different interests. The problem is, however, that competition in telecommunications does not deliver 'Christmas presents for all':

● Access to a telephone line - connection and rental charges - has been historically subsidised by usage of it: a subsidy accentuated as technology has further diminished the relative cost of transmission.

● High-volume business customers are far more profitable for telecommunications operators than low-volume residential customers, and initially benefited substantially more from competition.

● Some residential customers and customer premises - particularly low-users and those in remote locations - are 'uneconomic' to serve: they either cost an operator to provide service, or offer a rate of return so low that no operator would provide service on normal commercial terms unless required to do so.

Since privatisation, almost all customers have seen their overall telephony costs fall, largely as a result of improved technology. But business customers' costs have fallen more than those of residential customers. 'Low users' have been protected by targeted rebates and, in spite of a formal commitment to allow access prices to rise closer to access costs, OFTEL has fought shy of permitting BT to rebalance prices between access and usage as much as it might, and seen fit to impose a ceiling on connection charges. This discrepancy is the basis of BT's 'access deficit', the unrecovered cost of BT providing access to customers who can then be served by any operator: a baneful source of dispute in the determination of interconnection prices.

I have argued above that regulation intended to stimulate competition in telecommunications should be reduced, to reflect the fact that a dynamic and competitive international market has developed in the industry. There is no equivalent case, however, for curtailing regulation designed to ensure the maintenance and extension of affordable telecommunications services to the community as a whole. Indeed, the great challenge for tomorrow's regulator should be to find ways of achieving this that can coexist with the dynamically expanding industry of which these public service functions remain a part.

Access to telecommunications in Britain has lagged behind the United States and some European countries. Today, some 90 per cent of households have a 'phone at home, and perhaps another 5 per cent wish they could afford one. New technology is offering new opportunities to provide access to telephony for groups that were previously excluded (for instance, through disability) and developing new services that may come to be regarded as part of the basic telecommunications service. The next decade should also see a dramatic expansion in the resources accessible through telephony - training, for example, and on-line information databases - to those who can afford to connect to the network and buy or rent the necessary hardware. The public service element of telecommunications needs to change to reflect these changing opportunities.

First, there should be a clear definition of what public service obligations are, and how they should develop in the light of changing technology and market circumstances.

Both OFTEL and the European Commission have been seeking to define universal service. At very least, it should include the availability of basic voice telephony to a satisfactory standard to everyone who reasonably demands it, at an affordable price. But the variables in that equation - how basic a service? how good a standard? how affordable a price? - should change in line with changes in the standard service expected by most citizens.

Second, the costs of public service obligations should be calculated, and regularly recalculated; and a straightforward mechanism, fair to all operators, established for funding them in future. Arcane accounting conventions like BT's access deficit do not provide an appropriate basis for refunding an operator for the costs concerned: indeed, the access deficit itself bears no direct relationship to the cost of universal service.

OFTEL has made a start at calculating the costs. Both OFTEL and the European Commission have also recently proposed that public service obligations should be financed through a universal service fund, from contributions made *pro rata* by all operators participating in the market. That would be fair and sensible. It recognises, in particular, two important principles:

● that, in a competitive market, the cost of obligations should be imposed on the industry as a whole, and not on a single operator - regardless of how those obligations are delivered in practice;

● and that obligations should be funded by the industry and not the Treasury, where they would always be vulnerable to public expenditure constraints.

Third, the regulator should promote affordable access by encouraging operators to offer easy-payment options to low-income subscribers and by keeping down the cost of access. Price caps will continue to be needed in this area, even when they cease to be necessary for the market as a whole.

The cost of providing telecommunications services has dropped substantially and will drop further as technology develops and transmission costs reduce. The volume of telecommunications usage will continue to grow rapidly in future. Economists may be able to justify rebalancing access charges upwards in these circumstances, in order more accurately to reflect the costs of service provision, but social justification is much more difficult to find.

Everyone should be able to benefit from falling costs. One way of ensuring this would be to maintain a price cap of RPI±0 per cent on access charges (rental and connection). Another - avoiding the somewhat artificial distinction between access and usage - might be to impose a price cap based on the average cost of the lowest decile residential bill. In any case, different options for payment to meet individual customer needs - for example, differently packaged bundles of access and usage, including some requiring no upfront payment for connection - could make an important contribution to improving access to telephony.

Fourth, the regulator and government should act to ensure that new services, as they develop, contribute to the general good and not merely that of individuals who can afford the necessary hard- and software.

In the United States, access to 'superhighway' services for all - all schools, all hospitals, all communities - is a key part of the government's National Information Infrastructure initiative. So it should be here, if we are to enable people to benefit for themselves and maximise their potential in society. Tomorrow's public service obligation should include the connection of public and community agencies to relevant new services, and the provision of access points to on-line services in libraries and community centres where they will be available to those who cannot afford a PC of their own.

Universal service is only part of the public utility side of telecommunications, but it symbolises a wider principle for regulation. Telecommunications companies can and should develop their services and their profitability in the new global marketplace that beckons them. But in doing so, they should not sell short the domestic consumers - residential *and* business - who depend on them for social interaction and commercial advantage, and look forward to benefiting from new services that can enhance their lives and businesses. Every customer should gain, and everyone should be able to afford to be a customer. Making that happen, while allowing telecommunications companies to maintain their entrepreneurial zeal, is at the heart of the regulator's art.

Conclusion

This paper has proposed a new approach to regulating telecommunications - one that looks forward to the converged, competitive communications industry of tomorrow rather than back to a lost era of state monopoly. It suggests a way forward: but all ways forward in the communications industry must carry a health warning. It really is not possible, in the current state of technological progress, to forecast the future in this industry. Flexibility and responsiveness to further change are vital.

I have tried to focus in this paper on a new framework for regulation which would be more flexible and appropriate for the time we can foresee. I have not attempted to deal with all the issues facing a future communications regulator. Within the next few years, he or she will have to consider many other issues. For example:

- European liberalisation, scheduled by 1998, will increase pressure for European, rather than national regulation - which may seem (but not necessarily be) more suitable for combining international business and public service priorities.

- The advent of multimedia services will greatly increase line usage for many residential customers, requiring a major rethink of tariffs, including the balance of access and usage charges. One option that might be considered is charging customers for bits transferred, rather than undifferentiated use of access time.

Other issues like these could be added, and will be as the months go by. The key point is this: no regulatory régime in communications can or should again be expected to last a decade. Tomorrow's technology, tomorrow's costs, tomorrow's customer aspirations, tomorrow's regulatory objectives will all differ from today's in ways we cannot predict. Regulation will remain necessary to ensure that public service is secure, but its purpose and its methods should never become frozen by the industry's past as has happened in the last decade.

Notes

1. Dr David Souter is an independent writer and consultant on telecommunications, regulation and employment issues. He is the author of 'A Stakeholder approach to Regulation' in *Regulating Our Utilities* (IPPR, London, 1994) and the author of *Telecoms Privatisation: the British Experiment* (PTTI, Geneva, 1992) and *Regulating Telecommunications: the British Experience* (PTTI, Geneva, 1994). For five years from 1989, he was Head of Research for the National Communications Union, the main trade union in the British telecommunications industry.

2. Others argue that future revenues lie in the residential market. See for example the response to the Oftel Consultation *A Framework for Effective Competition*, by Cristina Murroni & Richard Collins of the IPPR Media Programme, *Interconnection, Universal Service and the Public Interest in UK Telecommunications*, available from IPPR.

3. 'A Stakeholder Approach to Regulation', in Dan Corry, David Souter and Michael Waterson, *Regulating Our Utilities*, Institute for Public Policy Research, 1994.

THE IMPLICATIONS OF COMPETITION
IN THE DOMESTIC GAS MARKET
PETER SPRING[1]

> "It's a mess. Deregulation and the rush to save a buck are
> combining to make victims of an estimated half-million
> Canadians. The problem, this time, is the natural gas
> brokers who sprang up after the government threw open
> the doors to the gas industry, allowing anyone with a
> shingle to sell the fuel. They can't get gas and the people
> who paid to earn the right for savings [on bills] are
> losing, big time."

Thus began a cautionary article in the Canadian *Citizen*[2] (headed
'Gas deregulation a fiasco') about the opening up to competition of
the domestic gas market - unique to date this century - initiated in
Eastern Canada at the end of the 1980s. Legislation currently going
through Parliament[3] to initiate a far more radical dismantling of the
domestic market monopoly in the UK has been presented purely as
technical and apolitical and appears to be broadly supported as such
by the three main parties. At the risk of sounding like Cassandra
some reservations might, however, be considered, as the UK enters
into the Brave New World of domestic gas market competition
buoyed on a wave of all-party consensus.

Domestic Gas Market Competition - A Unique Experiment

The expectation has developed that - once the domestic gas
monopoly has gone - anyone who switches from British Gas (BG)
to another supplier, and pays on time, will be charged 10 per cent
less (plus or minus 2 per cent depending on the distance from east
coast gas landing terminals). That the monopoly should be lifted is
presented as, in itself, nothing particularly untoward.

Yet monopoly up to now has been regarded as the natural state of
domestic gas supply. North America has pioneered competition in

commercial gas supply but even this is largely a development of the last 15 years. In the first quarter of the nineteenth century, a period of unfettered capitalism, gas supply in the UK monopolised:

> "With the growing demand for gas, new companies had sprung up throughout the nineteenth century. The streets of London became an obstacle course. ... There were pitched battles between the workmen of rival companies, who were forever fracturing and tapping each other's mains. As early as 1821, the gas companies had followed the example of the water industry and agreed to a division of London."[4]

This rather pre-dates the year 1847 mentioned by the President of the Board of Trade, Michael Heseltine in his speech[5] introducing the Gas Bill.

> "The assumption that the supply of gas to the public can best be undertaken on a monopoly basis dates from 1847, when a committee of inquiry led to the passing of the first Gasworks Clauses Act. The conclusion that monopoly was the necessary form of organisation was based on the poor economics of laying competing pipelines and the associated disruption in terms of street works that was found to entail."

Historically natural monopolisation largely preceded legislation. In the USA, a strongly free market economy, domestic gas is almost entirely supplied by local distribution companies (LDCs). In California, for example, there are two very large LDCs, Southern California (Socal) in the south and Pacific General & Electric (PG&E) in the central and northern areas. Independent gas marketers (IGMs) have a complex relationship with such LDCs, both selling the LDCs gas transported to California on interstate pipelines and using the LDCs' pipelines to distribute gas to their own large industrial customers. Most US independents, however, do not operate in the residential and small commercial market as the volumes taken by individual consumers are too small. As stated by

Shell UK in its evidence to the MMC[6]: 'Even in the USA, where gas market liberalisation and the associated regulation of gas transportation and storage had been taken the furthest, *local distribution monopolies remained a feature of the system*'. [writer's italics].

The only market where - the writer is aware - domestic gas competition has taken off this century is Eastern Canada. Even here gas distribution remains broadly the responsibility of the local utilities who continue to be responsible for billing and for managing safety. Gas brokers promised rebates to consumers, based on their ability to buy gas put into inter-provincial pipelines more cheaply than the utilities. To continue the quote taken earlier from the Canadian *Citizen*.[7]

> "Let's back up a bit. Deregulation was supposed to mean several things. Cheap gas and competition for the big guys.

> Independent companies would be able to sell natural gas directly to customers. They would use the delivery system already in place, whether Consumers Gas [the local utility] liked it or not. The advantage to home owners would be cheaper gas because the middleman was being cut out.

> It was all too simple. First, too many independents tried to get into the business. Some were simply out-and-out frauds. After pocketing $50 memberships they disappeared. Second, the scheme was marketed door-to-door. Remember all those salespeople trying to sign you up?

> All the companies promised substantial savings in the form of rebates at the end of each heating season. Sales pitches hinted at savings of up to $100. Reality has shown the rebates, when they are given, are in the $15 to $20 range...

> Last winter [1992/93] reality took over. Natural gas prices began an upward spiral that hasn't levelled off. The independents couldn't afford the gas. The big utilities can... Since then the dollar signs have been preceded by minus signs."

At least, however, in Canada the market has been trusted. In the UK, the irony is that it may be controlled - the term is 'pro-competitive regulation' - to try to ensure that 'competition' is a great success for ideological and political reasons.

Again quoting at some length, this time from a speech to the Oil Industries Club by John Collins, then chairman of and chief executive of Shell UK[8], which provides a succinct justification of domestic market monopoly:

> "The transmission and distribution infrastructure safely delivered gas to 80 per cent of British households as well as commercial and industrial customers. The technical problems involved in guaranteeing fluctuating supplies should not be underestimated. They required BG to maintain load balancing capacity, partly through its 'interruptible' supply contracts with industry. Safely managing such a system with many competing suppliers, and a separate transportation utility, would be much more complex and expensive.

> "Of course it would please domestic consumers if competition meant their gas cost less. But perhaps not if, as a consequence, the integrity of the gas supply system was prejudiced. I suggest that existing arrangements, whereby BG has a monopoly of such customers with an obligation to supply them, serve well, and I question whether - given the very real practical difficulties involved - liberalisation would provide significant additional benefits.

"I am not convinced that the practical problems of safely
and efficiently managing a liberalised mass gas market
have yet been overcome. The sensible and pragmatic
approach is to change only those aspects of the system
which are deficient. That is to open the large commercial
and industrial markets to free competition, as has been
happening."

As part of the Royal Dutch/Shell Group, the largest non-state owned
international gas operator, the concerns of Shell UK might have
carried some weight.

The UK is pioneering developments in domestic gas supply that are
largely without precedent - and seemingly with very little informed
public debate. Switching supplier from BG is presented as a simple
matter bringing seemingly riskless reward for as long as bills are
paid on time. What motivates such developments - experience or
ideology?

The Competition Emphasis - Ideologically Driven?

Developments in the UK gas industry are possibly incomprehensible
to the *traditional* analyst of international gas markets, if the
ideology which drives them in this country is ignored.

The story of British Gas (BG) since privatisation has been the
recovery of control of the agenda by economists styled 'Austrian'.
Put simply their belief is that the state is perforce coercive, at best
debilitating at worst corruptible and corrupting, and rather than rely
on it individuals must make choices, seen as 'positive public
choice'. From this it follows that monopoly, whether nationalised or
privatised, is by definition damaging as it denies choice. Monopoly
must be cut down to size, where it cannot be abolished, and
competition promoted. The argument is as much driven by morality
as by the belief that competition is invariably more efficient than
monopoly, whether state or privately owned. (Where state ownership
continues an 'internal' market should be created - as in the NHS or
BBC.)

The role of a small group of academics in the remodelling of BG (indeed the shape of Britain) has not been sufficiently credited. Three deserve particular recognition, Professors Colin Robinson, Michael Beesley and Stephen Littlechild who, apart from their other roles, are respectively editorial director, a managing trustee and academic advisory council member of the Institute of Economic Affairs (IEA). Consider a seminal paper written by Stephen Littlechild, now of OFFER, in October 1981 titled *Ten Steps to Denationalisation.*[9] This set out ten 'suggestions' for nationalised industries covering, apart from gas, electricity, telecommunications, post, rail, coal and other state owned transport, manufacturing and commercial concerns. The Government has proved highly suggestible: the suggestions are now largely fact. A paper *The regulation of privatised monopolies in the United Kingdom*[10] published in 1989 by Stephen Littlechild and Michael Beesley, his mentor at Birmingham University in the 1960s, discusses BG in terms of its separate 'distribution', 'transmission' and 'supply' functions, although these had not been recognised in its privatisation structure.

Before privatisation, BG was an extraordinary operation - almost a kingdom within a kingdom. It had a monopsony over gas purchasing and a monopoly *de jure* over domestic and *de facto* over business sales. It could lay pipes bypassing planning procedure, dig up streets, and break and enter property to check for gas leaks or suspected meter tampering. Between 1960 and 1986 it increased gas market share from just over 5 per cent to over 40 per cent of final energy consumption as the result of exploitation of North Sea gas reserves and the construction of an efficient, integrated, high pressure transmission system which, despite the large variation between average and winter UK peak demand, operated by international comparison on low levels of storage.

By the standards of prevailing free-market economics the pre-privatised BG was highly incorrect. Yet to a remarkable degree it was, on privatisation, translated intact into the private sector in 1986: this being the price of the co-operation of the board, led by Sir Denis Rooke, with a 100 per cent rapid sale during the run-up to the 1987 general election. A supplementary memorandum[11] submitted to the Energy Committee after publication of the 1986 Gas Bill, written by Professor Colin Robinson of Surrey University and his wife Dr Eileen Marshall reflected the hostility of free-market academics. This stated: 'The government's proposals are ill-considered and over-influenced by a desire to raise substantial revenue quickly.' A constantly repeated theme came later: 'It is most unlikely that any significant gas-to-gas competition will appear in the industrial market [a prognostication which has proved wrong] so long as British Gas owns and operates the pipelines.' And:

> "If the proposals go through the Parliament in their present form, an opportunity will have been missed and an unfortunate precedent will have been set for other energy industries where more competition could have been introduced but which, like gas, may well see advantages in becoming private rather than state monopolies."

Indeed the proposals did go through largely unchanged, except for the Portillo amendment which gave the Director-General of OFGAS the duty to enable effective competition for gas supplies in the market exceeding 25,000 therms - the level above which BG's monopoly ceased.[12]

Post-Privatisation - the Grip Tightens?

In 1987, within a year of privatisation and after a general election, BG's commercial (contract) business was referred to the Monopolies and Mergers Commission (MMC) by the Director-General of the Office of Fair Trading (DGFT). BG's practice of negotiating individual contracts - in effect perfect price discrimination - in the firm contract market (that is the market to business users without dual-fuel burners which would enable them to switch between gas and oil), while economically efficient hardly endeared itself to such customers. The MMC's 1988 report[13] concluded that:

"The gains [from its recommendations, principally the publication of price schedules which competitors, but not BG, could undercut] will be more significant than the losses and that our proposals will contribute towards the emergence of effective competition in gas supply. It is only through such competition that a long-term solution can be found to the adverse effects we [one of the MMC panellists was Littlechild] have identified in our inquiry."

At the Conservative Party conference in 1991 the ending of BG's domestic monopoly was put on the agenda by the then Secretary of State at the Department of Trade and Industry Peter Lilley. In 1992 BG was referred to the MMC again by the Director-General of OFGAS, Sir James Mckinnon, over the issue of BG's ownership of the pipeline and storage system, which, perhaps understandably from its point of view, it wanted to continue as it constituted 90 per cent of its UK asset base. This reference was trumped by a broader reference by DTI Secretary of State Michael Heseltine into all aspects of the UK gas market. The MMC's headline conclusion[14] was that:

"BG's conduct in undertaking its business as an integrated business, and its failure to provide for neutrality as between its trading and transportation interests, may be expected to reduce the effectiveness of competition and to operate against the public interest by inhibiting choice, restricting innovation, and leading to higher levels of gas prices than would otherwise be the case. ... We recommend that the adverse effects identified should be remedied by divestment of BG's trading [not pipelines and storage] no later than 31 March 1997 [the panellist with responsibility for structure was Beesley]."

The MMC did not, however, find the domestic monopoly against the public interest: 'We do not believe that BG's conduct in operating its monopoly of supply to the tariff [domestic] market is against the public interest'.[15] It did, however, recommend its gradual removal (almost against the thrust of its general argument - indeed read textually it is a peculiarly schizophrenic document), starting with the reduction in the tariff threshold from 2,500 to 1,500 therms per annum, following divestment of trading in 1997. Complete removal should only take place 3 to 5 years afterwards and only following the most careful consideration of the effects. The MMC did not deny that there might be losers:

> "BG's logical response to competition would be to rebalance its tariffs to reflect the structure of its costs and restore its profits, also reducing the scope for competitors to undercut BG. Supply to lower-volume users (whose use of gas may be confined to cookers or water heaters and who probably include a high proportion of elderly and poor customers) is currently unprofitable, and may require significant price increases."

Only when the full MMC report was published several weeks later, including evidence submitted by the DTI,[16] was it apparent to what extent the MMC had ignored the DTI's views. For example:

> "The Government was committed to the removal of the tariff threshold. ... Separation of ownership of transportation and sales would be a similarly complex exercise with its own transitional uncertainties. It seems unlikely both could be attempted in parallel."

> "Actual implementation of the threat [of break-up] would end BG's present ability to underpin the market during transition. ... It would no doubt be seen by some BG shareholders as a break with the spirit of the 1986 regime and the sale prospectus."

The DTI repaid the compliment and its response to the MMC recommendations was to largely ignore them, taking break-up off the agenda and putting the early introduction of domestic market competition back on it.

Sir James Mckinnon had announced his resignation soon after the second MMC reference was made in 1992. This was to take effect a year later, twelve months before completion of his second term of office. He was replaced by Ms Clare Spottiswoode who had been a tutor in the London Business School's (LBS) Centre for Enterprise, specialising in small businesses. In January 1994 it was announced that Eileen Marshall would assume the newly created post of chief economic adviser at OFGAS, having been Director of Regulation and Business Affairs at OFFER reporting to Professor Littlechild. Professor Beesley was appointed a consultant to OFGAS in August last year.[17]

Despite the fact that the MMC jointly did not consider the domestic monopoly to be against the public interest - and anyway recommended that its removal should only take place gradually and with the most careful consideration of the consequences - legislation is now underway to remove the BG's domestic monopoly faster than recommended by the MMC. What might be the consequences?

What Might Competition Mean for the Domestic Gas Market?

It is frequently stated that because IGMs have undercut BG by 10 per cent in industrial and commercial markets they will do so in the domestic market once the monopoly is lifted. The comparison, however, is false[18] and in appraising the implications of a competitive domestic market certain factors should not be overlooked:

● *Lower prices in commercial market not relevant to domestic market*: Before the introduction of competition in the commercial market this subsidised the domestic market. Margins were high and there were plenty of 'cherries' to pick. Following the introduction of competition, margins in the commercial market have been driven down. Margins in the domestic market have not been fat. It is, therefore, dangerous to argue that because price cuts were large in the commercial market domestic users will automatically see 10 per cent price cuts.

● *Limited domestic market margin for IGMs to undercut*: A gas marketer's costs - whether that of BG's own Public Gas Supplier (PGS) business unit or that of an IGM - only account for about 15 per cent (see the Appendix) of the domestic consumer's bill. The rest is transportation and storage costs (where charges will be the same for everyone) and gas costs (where there will be some variation). Therefore, IGMs will broadly have to be able to undercut BG PGS's own cost structure by two thirds, to be able to deliver average 10 per cent price cuts.

● *Industry costs increased by new entry*: The domestic gas market - unlike telecom markets which are rapidly growing and where new technology is constantly being developed - is at best expanding very slowly and might contract if conservation takes off. If unit volume sales are static and competition is to result in lower unit prices then the total revenue generated by the industry must fall. New entrants will, however, bring in their own costs, much of which will duplicate that of the incumbent. To the extent that the incumbent does not or cannot shed costs, a painful and politically unpopular process, total costs in the industry will rise and its profitability fall or its prices will rise. (The costs of entry into the domestic market will be high in terms of advertising, provision of financial guarantees, securing adequate supplies of gas, and installing mass information technology (IT) systems.)

● *Information Technology*: The sheer complexity of the IT issue has almost certainly not received the attention it deserves. The reduction of the monopoly threshold in both gas and electricity has always been accompanied by furious complaints of duplicate, incorrect, or non billing. The manifesto of some IGMs, mostly RECs associated with United Gas, titled *Wouldn't you just love to be in control* (better known by the name given to it by the Gas Consumers Council - *The Rupert Bear Annual*, 'being short on numbers but long on words and pictures') asserted that they could cut the annual costs of meter reading from £11.54 to £3.60 because they were much more efficient. But one should note experience in the sector so far. As of April 1st 1994 the electricity market for consumers with a peak load of 100 kWh and above, roughly 25,000 therms, was opened up to competition. The extension of competition from about 10,000 to 50,000 consumers produced a metering crisis. The IT problems of a competing mass gas or electricity market have not yet been tackled and could prove horrendous.

- *Safety and access to property*: Cordless phones are fine but pipeless gas is not. The safety problem is real as gas does not 'fail-safe'. Unlike electricity, if gas supply to an area is cut, engineers have to ensure all appliances are shut-off before supply is resumed. Gas companies around the world have draconian powers to break and enter to make safe gas leaks. In a competitive market would such powers proliferate and could domestic safety be secured?

- *Domestic market cross-subsidy*: In a competitive market in the long run no one will be supplied if the individual marginal cost of supplying him or her (let alone any share of overhead costs) is not covered by the marginal revenue he or she generates. There are currently many layers of domestic market cross-subsidy, depending on:

  - *volume* (therms per year) consumed;
  - *load* (the relationship between highest and average daily consumption);
  - *location* (town or country, east or west);
  - and *administrative cost* (depending on whether direct debit, standing order, pre-payment, cash, on-time or late).

Sensitivities about the volume and location cross-subsidies can to some extent be dissipated by locking them in TransCo (BG's transportation and storage business). The load cross-subsidy paradoxically favours larger volume users, as generally these have central heating systems and 'peakier' loads, at the expense of low volume users.

Administrative costs vary enormously: it costs very little to service a consumer paying by direct debit and a great deal to chase a slow or unreliable payer (possibly through no fault of his or her own) to the point of disconnection. The issue is sensitive as seen in the criticism of 'discounts' for direct debit. These are not really discounts but a shift towards cost-reflective pricing which has further to go. In the long run cross-subsidies must be exposed and eliminated by competition, either because BG rebalances or because, if prevented, it withdraws and new entrants charge cost-reflective pricing.

The problem is that cost-reflective pricing, the official policy, conflicts with the political necessity of presenting competition without losers.

OFGAS have made the position clear:

> "It is already a key element of the Government's energy policy, set out in the March 1993 White Paper (Cm 2235) 'that service is provided to customers in a commercial environment in which customers pay the full [ie. accounting not economic] cost of the energy resources they consume.'"[19]

BG's transportation and storage business TransCo, established that the cost-reflective charge for the domestic customers' actual site costs (as opposed to the cost of actual pipelining to the site) should be composed of two elements: a fixed charge of £26.08 a year and a variable charge of 2.48 pence per therm consumed. But OFGAS set out the following modification on 30th September 1994 in a document entitled *Annex 1: Approval of Methodology*:[20]

> The substitution for the words:
> "Fixed £26.08 per annum; Variable 2.48 pence per therm"
> ... of the words:
> "Fixed £15.00 per annum; Variable 4.19 pence per therm".

Table 1 shows the effect of this OFGAS determination:

Table 1
Domestic Site Charges Under TransCo Price Proposals
and OFGAS' Determination

Therms/Year Consumed	44	650	1550
(£)			
TransCo Pricing Proposal			
Fixed Element (£26.08/year)	26.08	26.08	26.08
Variable Element (2.48p/therm)	1.09	16.12	38.44
Total Annual Site Charge	**27.17**	**42.20**	**64.52**
OFGAS Determination			
Fixed Element (£15.00/Year)	15.00	15.00	15.00
Variable Element (4.19p/therm)	1.84	27.24	64.95
Total Annual Site Charge	**16.84**	**42.24**	**79.95**

Under the proposal by BG TransCo, the difference between the site charge for the 44 and 1550 therm site was £37.35 (£64.52 *less* £27.17) - this difference being something of a mystery in itself as the meters and service pipe supplying all domestic users are the same. Under the OFGAS determination the difference is a larger £63.11 (£79.95 *less* £16.84) which is even more mysterious. It does, however, have the advantageous effect of reducing the relative cost to marketing companies of transporting gas for low volume users.

In November 1994 the Trade and Industry Committee report into opening the domestic gas market commented that the setting of a £15 site charge and a 4.19p variable charge:

> "appears to involve an element of cross-subsidy from large to small users. This is contrary to the Government's preference for cost-reflective energy prices. It would be unacceptable if, without this being made explicit, cross-subsidies were put in place simply to facilitate the transition to a competitive market, only to be removed subsequently. OFGAS plans to review the division between the fixed and variable costs in 1997. *We are*

concerned by the possibility of some manipulation of the transportation site charge at a later stage, and seek some assurances from the Government and OFGAS on this matter.[21]

The charge of cross-subsidy elicited the following response from OFGAS:[22]

"Having calculated a range of figures, we considered the impact of a particular standing charge on the prospects for competition in supply. We therefore selected a number that was towards the lower end of the range of our scenarios - hence £15. At this level, the standing charge continues to contribute towards the cost of service pipes, metering, data collection, and emergency service."

It seems clear then that subjective decisions aimed at promoting the smooth and uncontroversial introduction of competition and ensuring its 'political' acceptability were the key to setting a fixed site charge of £15.00 in place of £26.08. This left a problem, however, as what to do about the 2.48 pence per therm variable site charge. OFGAS explained:

"TransCo has a right to recover the full amount of revenue to which it is entitled under the terms of the price formula. Necessarily it follows that TransCo is entitled to recover any shortfall in revenue caused by increasing the charge per therm that it levies.

Accordingly the Director General specified that TransCo was entitled to recover the costs which it described as 'customer-related' through a £15 standing charge and the remainder as a 4.19 pence per therm. This does not mean that the Director General accepted the costs described by the TransCo as 'customer related' are accurately and properly described, merely that TransCo was entitled to recover these costs."

In the document *Annex 1: Approval of Methodology* referred to earlier, OFGAS itself had set the 4.19 pence per therm variable site charge. Why did it do so if it is not accepted that such costs 'are accurately and properly described'? There is clearly a cross-subsidy because large volume users have higher site charges than lower volume users - although such site costs are in practice essentially the same - and it looks as though OFGAS has increased a cross-subsidy originally put in place by TransCo.[23]

The question then becomes will the cross-subsidy be maintained? The comments in the debate on the Gas Bill[24] are ambiguous.

> **Mr Richard Caborn** (Sheffield, Central): ... Both the right hon. Gentleman and the regulator accept the figure of £15. Can he give assurances that the cross-subsidy, which is now built into the price, will continue and that it will not be removed in the near future?

> **Mr Heseltine:** The hon. Gentleman puts the case very fairly, in asking about the £15 standard charge that it is built into the proposals. That matter is subject in the end to the regulatory regime, but obviously there would be no point in changing the regime shortly after it had been introduced. I am sure that the hon. Gentleman will be reassured by the answer I have given.

This could be taken to mean that 'the cross-subsidy which is now built into the price, will continue and that it will not be removed in the near future' because 'there would be no point in changing the regime shortly after it had been introduced'. This would then constitute an assurance in response to the Trade and Industry Committee's concern about 'the possibility of some manipulation of the transportation site charge at some later stage.'[25]

Conclusion

A number of issues have been outlined, reflecting the problems which might have been fully discussed when considering the legislation for the most public current gas industry 'big issue', that is domestic market competition.

There is a general perception that everyone will have a choice of supplier and that such choice can only produce winners. Price reductions for some may, however, be at the expense of rises for others - a point it seems not generally grasped. Indeed, on the basis of available information it is difficult to avoid the conclusion that low volume users will pay higher prices in a competitive market (see the Appendix).

The pilot scheme may provide some insights into BG PGS's and the IGM's pricing policies. In the year starting 1st April 1996 an area covering 500,000 consumers will be opened to competition. In the following year this will be extended to 2 million households. Cornwall, Devon and Somerset will provide the area for the first trial. Cornwall and Somerset are represented in the European Parliament by Liberal Democrats and Devon would almost certainly have been but for the dubious intervention of a Literal Democrat.

There are two schools of thought about the choice of area: firstly, that it will be hailed as a great success for competition policy which will be used against the Liberal Democrats in the south west. Or that it won't be a great success as it will become clear that choice will lie with the supplier not with the consumer and many will face higher rebalanced prices; or because the scheme may collapse because the IT problems are insuperable in the permitted timeframe - therefore, it might be best to keep as far away from London as possible, in areas where Conservatives expect to lose seats anyway.

The first stage of the pilot scheme may not, however, give very realistic results. It will be conducted using the current TransCo charging system which will be replaced as of April 1st 1997. Also, the trial will cover a very limited proportion of the population, and in a pre-election trial period, marketers may not behave as profit-maximisers.

On the basis of present polls an election will produce a change in Government which would almost certainly lead to changes in regulatory policy and personnel. It is probably realistic to say that there would be less emphasis on promoting competition *per se* and greater consideration of the implications of competition for all consumers - without the ideological conviction[26] that competition invariably produces superior results: indeed could be wasteful in certain industries. The options will be:

● discontinue the current policy as outlined in the Gas Bill and see domestic monopoly restored possibly on a regional or even a franchise basis;

● continue the current scheme:

  - and let the incumbent rebalance prices - in which case cost reflective pricing by PGS will produce winners and losers;

  - and prevent the incumbent from rebalancing - in which case PGS will suffer from 'cherry-picking' in the higher volume sectors of the market. The loss of such custom would eventually make its ability to supply lower volume users, who do not cover costs, unsustainable - resulting in its withdrawal from the domestic gas market and its replacement by IGMs who would charge cost-reflective prices.

The social and political implications of price rebalancing will eventually have to be seriously addressed: it will not be sufficient to rely indefinitely on the incumbent continuing to supply lower volume users at non-cost reflective prices while incomers 'cherry-pick' the higher volume consumers. If policy is not to be socially divisive choices then become:

● a return to regulated monopoly and uniform prices;

● a competitive market[27] with a comprehensive industry levy
  which means that the cost of supply to low volume and more
  disadvantaged users is met by the industry as a whole. Although
  there is provision for a levy in the legislation, OFGAS and the
  IGMs have shown little enthusiasm for one, seeing the cost as
  raising barriers to entry and seemingly preferring such costs to
  be borne by BG's shareholders.[28]

At the beginning there was an apology for being a Cassandra
(anyway no-one listened to Cassandra). What, however, should not
go unrecognised is that the Gas Bill fundamentally changes the
nature of gas supply. Competition breaks the 'utility compact'
whereby all domestic consumers, regardless of levels of
consumption, within a certain distance from an existing pipeline, are
supplied at a uniform price and level of service standard. In a
competitive market each user has got to generate revenue to cover
his or her marginal cost of supply - plus over time a proportionate
share of administrative overhead - whether through his or her own
payment or because that payment is supplemented by a levy. It is
very questionable whether gas consumers are aware of the
fundamental nature of this change.

Appendix

The Appendix sets out a detailed analysis of transportation and storage costs in the domestic market. It is from this that the writer's views about the implications of competition for the ending of cross-subsidies and overall prices in the domestic market are developed. The detail should enable critics of the writer's analysis to correct any of his errors and provide a substitute analysis. Sufficient pricing information is, however, now available to begin to quantify the implications of a shift to a competitive domestic gas market. First, however, a base case for domestic prices needs to be established. Table IA shows the 'base model' calculation of transportation charges. It assumes roughly average points of 'entry' and 'exit' for the National Transmission System (NTS) for the 650 therm consumer. Also it uses the target price for the Regional System, as of October 1997, when planned rises have been fully phased in over 3 years. (In practice these prices may be superseded by the 1997 TransCo formula review but they do represent the position towards which TransCo is trying to move.)

Table IA
Transportation & Storage Charges for 650 Therms/Year Consumer

	p/pdth/a*	load factor	Pence/ Therm	Therm/ Year	£ Year
National Transmission System					
Capacity					
- *Entry (average)*	81.00*	0.36	0.62	650	4.01
- *Exit (average)*	106.00*	0.36	0.81	650	5.24
Commodity			1.05	650	6.82
Regional System**					
Capacity	739.80*	0.36	5.63	650	36.60
Commodity			5.03	650	32.67
Delivery Requirement (storage)					
Commodity			2.40	650	15.60
Customer (site variable)					
Commodity			4.19	650	27.24
Total Variable Charge			**19.72**	**650**	**128.17**
Customer (site fixed)					
fixed			2.31	650	15.00
Total			**22.03**	**650**	**143.17**

* *pence per peak day therm per annum (eg: 81.00/0.36/365=0.62)*
** *target for October 1997*

Table IIA shows the structure of end user prices for the average user of 650 therms per annum. This is based on charges as of January 1 1995 to users not paying by direct debit. It also shows the amounts recovered from 18 million tariff consumers.

Table IIA
Estimated Structure of Domestic Market Costs for BG PGS

	Pence/ Therm	Therm/ Year	£/ Year	Customers (million)	£m
Transportation and Storage Costs					
Customer Costs					
Site Charges					
- Fixed	2.31		15.00	18	270
- Variable	4.19	650	27.24	18	490
Total Site Charges	6.50		42.24	18	760
Usage Costs Commodity	15.53	650	100.94	18	1817
Total TransCo Costs	**22.03**		**143.17**	**18**	**2577**
Gas Costs Commodity	**20.00**	**650**	**130.00**	**18**	**2340**
Marketer's Own Costs					
Non-gas Costs Fixed	6.66		43.30	18	779
Imputed Profits Capacity	0.86		5.56	18	100
Commodity	0.85	650	5.53	18	100
Marketer's Imputed Profits	**1.71**		**11.09**	**18**	**200**
End-User Prices	**50.39**		**327.56**	**18**	**5896**

Certain assumptions have been made in Table IIA.

● Gas costs are 20p per therm. Gas is currently changing hands on the informal 'spot' market for 14p to 16p as there is currently a surplus. It is doubtful, however, whether a long term domestic gas business, with its absolute security of supply requirement, could be built on the basis of spot purchases. Eastern Canada showed the risk here.

● The profit estimated from domestic marketing is about £200 million spread across 18 million users. It is assumed that this is 50 per cent capacity and 50 per cent commodity related although in practice the capacity element is probably higher. Profit from the average user is about £11 per household, split £5.56 per consumer and 0.85p per therm. These are highly notional figures but some assumptions have to be made because, in a competitive market, in the long run no consumer will be supplied unless he is deemed individually profitable.

● Non-gas charges represent the cost to the marketer which is established initially as a residual after TransCo, gas costs and profits are deducted from the sales price. Non-gas costs are basically fixed as it costs the same to bill customers using the same payment method, regardless of consumption. In practice unit non-gas costs may rise for BG as it loses market share to the extent that it cannot cut fixed costs. For competing marketers they will be extremely high initially both because of start-up costs, costs of persuading people to switch supplier; and because they will be spread across a small - if growing - customer base. (This implies that costs in a business with little volume growth could rise - so industry profits may fall.)

At present it seems to be the simplistic view that after competition is introduced prices charged (ex. VAT) will be as set out in Table IIIA for British Gas and its competitors.

The Table compares the following:

-   British Gas' prices as increased on January 1 1995.

-   British Gas' prices to direct debit consumers as of January 1 1995.

-   Prices in *Wouldn't you just love to be in control?* which simply cut the pre-January 1st 1995 BG standing charge from £36.88 to £32.00 and the commodity charge from 43.30p per therm to 40.00p per therm. As a bigger percentage cut is made in the standing charge than the commodity charge smaller volume users apparently receive larger relative price cuts compared with BG price cuts.

- The OFGAS/DTI joint consultation document *The choice of areas for the initial extension of further competition into the gas market* says:

> "The independent gas suppliers have said that following the introduction of competition they will be able to offer savings of around 10 per cent on average to domestic consumers. However, within the pattern of the benefits of competition, there may be small regional variations of around +/-2 per cent of final prices, to the extent that suppliers pass through changes in the transportation prices."

This appears rather a dangerous assumption but it is in the document.

Table IIIA: Domestic Gas Prices

Therms/year consumed	44	650	1550
(£)			
British Gas			
Standing Charge (£37.95/year)	37.95	37.95	37.95
Commodity Charge (44.56p/therm)	19.60	289.61	690.61
Total Annual Bill	**57.55**	**327.56**	**728.56**
British Gas Direct Debit			
Standing Charge (£36.88/year)	36.88	36.88	36.88
Commodity Charge (42.00p/therm)	18.48	273.01	651.02
Total Annual Bill	**55.36**	**309.89**	**687.90**
Wouldn't You Just Love to be in Control?			
Standing Charge (£32.00/year)	32.00	32.00	32.00
Commodity Charge (40.00p/therm)	17.60	260.00	620.00
Total Annual Bill	**49.60**	**292.00**	**652.00**
OFGAS/DTI			
Consultation Document*			
Standing Charge (£34.16/year)	34.16	34.16	34.16
Commodity Charge (40.10p/therm)	17.64	260.64	621.54
Total Annual Bill	**51.80**	**294.80**	**655.79**

* *on regional trials*

Looking at the four cross-subsidies identified in the main text:

● *Load (the relationship between average demand over the year and demand on days which is high due to cold weather)* - There is an imputed load factor of 36 per cent which effectively covers the domestic market; so in practice small volume users - as they generally don't have central heating - tend paradoxically to subsidise large volume users.

● *Location* - Since the May 1994 publication of the OFGAS document *Competition and choice in the gas market* there have been changes have been made in NTS entry/exit charges which reduce the regional disparity. Comparing Devonshire and Cornwall with South Humberside as exit points, and using notional unchanged average entry points, the differences in prices emerge using the pro-forma model - as shown in Table IVA.

Table IVA: Changes in Regional Variations
Therms/year consumption is 650

Region	Devonshire & Cornwall	South Humberside	Regional Variation
June Proposals (£)	338.29	322.51	+/- 2.45%
July Proposals (£)	334.83	323.95	+/- 1.68%

It appears that regional variations are a bit of a red herring - despite the political concern - but more extreme examples could be found by comparing, for example, St Fergus entry and South West exit with Easington entry and South Humberside exit.

● *Volume* - This is the key cross-subsidy and could prove highly politically sensitive when exposed. In a competitive market every consumer will have to pay a price that individually covers his costs and provides a profit margin. Table VA shows rebalanced prices for BG assuming no cross-subsidy except that already built into TransCo. In a competitive market in the long run BG will have no choice but to rebalance or withdraw. Either way low volume users will pay more.

Table VA
Estimated Rebalanced Cost-reflective BG Prices

		Pence/ Therm	£/ Year
650 Therm/year consumer			
Total TransCo Costs		22.03	143.17
Gas Costs	Commodity	20.00	130.00
Non-gas Costs	Fixed	6.66	43.30
Marketer	Profits	1.71	11.09
End-user	**Prices**	**50.39**	**327.56**
44 Therm/year Consumer			
Total TransCo Costs		53.81	23.68
Gas Costs	Commodity	20.00	8.80
Non-gas Costs	Fixed	98.40	43.30
Marketer	Profits	13.49	5.93
End-user	**Prices**	**185.70**	**81.71**
1550 Therm/year Consumer			
Total TransCo Costs		20.69	320.64
Gas Costs	Commodity	20.00	310.00
Non-gas Costs	Fixed	2.79	43.30
Marketer	Profits	1.21	18.75
End User	**Prices**	**44.69**	**692.69**

Independents claim that they will be able to undercut BG. In Table VIA the margin available to cover non-gas costs and profits is shown assuming: no rebalancing by BG; that independents actually charge the prices which they claim they will and; everyone pays the same TransCo and gas costs.

What should become clear is that there is very little margin particularly at the lower volume end of the market. Also, unless the independents have much lower gas costs than BG, then on their and OFGAS' proposed prices there is precious little margin anyway.

Inevitably IGMs - for perfectly understandable commercial reasons - will avoid the low volume users who do not pay cost-reflective prices and focus on high volume users. Eventually lower volume users will have to pay rebalanced prices to either IGMs or British Gas. It is hard to avoid the conclusion that there will eventually be losers in absolute terms from competition.

Table VIA
Margin to Cover Non-gas Costs and Profits

Therms/yr Offtake	44	180	650	1000	1550
(£)					
British Gas					
TransCo and Gas costs	32.48	86.49	273.17	412.19	630.64
Non-gas costs & Profit Margin	**25.07**	**31.66**	**54.39**	**71.32**	**97.92**
Total Annual Bill	57.55	118.15	327.56	483.51	728.56
British Gas Direct Debit					
TransCo and Gas costs	32.48	86.49	273.17	412.19	630.64
Non-gas costs & Profit Margin	**22.88**	**25.99**	**36.72**	**44.70**	**57.26**
Total Annual Bill	55.36	112.48	309.89	456.89	687.90
Wouldn't you just love to be in control?					
TransCo and Gas Costs	32.48	86.49	273.17	412.19	630.64
Non-gas Costs & Profit Margin	**17.12**	**17.51**	**18.83**	**19.81**	**21.36**
Total Annual Bill	49.60	104.00	292.00	432.00	652.00
OFGAS/DTI Consultation Document*					
TransCo and Gas costs	32.48	86.49	273.17	412.19	630.64
Non-gas costs & Profit Margin	**19.32**	**19.85**	**21.63**	**22.97**	**25.06**
Total Annual Bill	51.80	106.43	294.80	435.16	655.70

* on the regional trials

● *Administrative costs* - The general line appears to be that only
the feckless will lose from competition (although the analysis
above does not support this view). There are clearly major
differences between the administrative cost of serving a direct
debit customer and chasing a consumer to the point of
disconnection - put as high as ten times. The point about
discounts for direct debit is that they are not discounts but a
move towards cost reflective pricing which has further to go.
Cash payers - no matter how timely - cost more and will
eventually pay more than those using direct debit. (These tend
to be lower volume and less well off users and even the
deserving poor may find it hard to pay on time.) In political
terms rebalancing in line with administrative costs could have
significant repercussions due to the coincidence of low volume
use with high administrative costs.

Notes

1. Peter Spring was an oil and gas analyst at Henderson
    Crosthwaite Institutional Brokers specialising in the UK and
    North American gas businesses since 1985. He now works in
    a consultancy role.

2. 'Gas deregulation a fiasco', *Citizen* 14.9.93.

3. This is a complex piece of legislation stripping British Gas of
    its domestic market monopoly. The complexity follows in part
    from the fact that competition in domestic gas supply was not
    envisaged in the 1986 Gas Act which effectively posited
    ownership of the pipeline and storage system in the sole Public
    Gas Supplier licencee which was British Gas. Hence the need
    for primary legislation to separate ownership of the physical
    system from operation as one of many sellers of gas to the
    domestic market. There seems to be a drip feed of main bill
    and then licences which has made it impossible to develop a
    coherent picture of the proposed changes in advance. Also, the
    licences allow considerable discretion to OFGAS in making
    marketers' terms more or less onerous.

4. To continue: "From then on the companies were authorised to
    dig up their own territory only, cutting up the thoroughfares
    with their narrow trenches and wrecking the streets with their
    shallow and badly laid pipes. This happy and chaotic state
    continued until 1873, when the first steamroller took to the
    roads of London and systematically flattened every pipe in its
    path. From then on, gas pipes had to be laid deeper and with
    more care - which meant more expensively." Safety is not
    necessarily cheap.

    R Trench and E Hillman, *London under London: A
    Subterranean Guide*, John Murray (Publishers) Ltd, 1984.

5. *Gas Bill, Parliamentary Debates*, Hansard, 13/3/ 1995.

6. *Gas; Volume 3.* The Monopolies and Mergers Commissions, Cm 2314, London: HMSO, 1993.

7. *op cit.*

8. *FT International Gas Report*, February 1993.

9. S.C. Littlechild, 'Ten Steps to Denationalisation', *Economic Affairs*, October 1981.

10. M.E.Beesley and S.C.Littlechild, 'The regulation of privatised monopolies in the United Kingdom', *Rand Journal of Economics*, Vol. 20, No. 3, Autumn 1989.

11. C.Robinson and E.Marshall, 'Regulation of the Gas Industry: Memorandum 28', *Regulation of the Gas Industry*, House of Commons Energy Committee, HC15-i, London, HMSO, November 1985.

12. The Central Electricity Generating Board (CEGB) was not to escape break-up becoming the Electricity Supply Industry (ESI), being correctly deconstructed into its generating, transmission, distribution and supply elements. This paper would be stepping into others' territory were it to comment on the ESI (or railways) but recent history has not proved the superiority of the deconstructed model compared with the more integrated British Telecoms or Gas model in terms either of raising revenue for the tax payer or extending choice of supplier to the consumer.

13. *Gas*, The Monopolies and Mergers Commission, Cm.500, London: HMSO, 1988.

14. *Gas; Volume 1*, The Monopolies and Mergers Commissions, Cm. 2314, London: HMSO, 1993.

15. *Ibid.* It is difficult to believe that the panel was entirely unified on all issues for textual analysis might suggest there followed

an interpolation: 'On the other hand, the disadvantages of monopoly and the benefits of competition cannot be fully predictable: competitors, could, for example, develop different product attributes, such as differentials between off-peak tariffs, the scope for which BG now regards as limited. An important economic benefit of abolition of the monopoly would be to bring cost-reflective prices, and more efficient allocation of resources.'

16. Gas; Volume 3. The Monopolies and Mergers Commissions, Cm .2314, London: HMSO, 1993.

17. MMC inquiry member joins OFGAS, *The Times*, 24/8/1994.

18. 'It is widely accepted that competition will reduce the overall level of prices ... The IGMs often quote the 10 per cent plus reductions experienced by both firm contract customers (>25,000 Th/yr) and large tariff customers (>2,500 Th/yr). Such comparisons are without merit as firstly, BG traditionally (pre-competition) enjoyed much higher margins from these customer groups than from domestic customers. Secondly, the IGMs have enjoyed essentially free load balancing services, courtesy of their gas transportation contracts which in effect have only required shippers to balance their loads on a monthly basis. Furthermore, there has been no effective monitoring that the load factors declared for individual customers are correct and cheating is widespread.'

Gas Strategies, 'Memorandum submitted by Gas Strategies', *The Domestic Gas Market*, House of Commons Trade and Industry Committee, HC15-II, London, HMSO, November 1994.

19. *Competition and Choice in the Gas Market*, OFGAS, May 1994.

In the light of denials that there has been a 'political fix' in setting a cross-subsidy in TransCo, as identified in November

1994 by the Trade and Industry Select Committee, it is interesting that the following comments were not criticised at the time.'At the heart of the document is a political fix: Gas's transportation arm will levy on both Gas's supply arm and its rivals an annual standing charge of £25 per customer. This level has been chosen so that, once the supply arm's fixed costs are taken into account, it will not have to put up its standing charge to customers of £37. So ministers need not worry about Granny facing a higher gas bill.' Lex, *The Financial Times*, 10/5/94.

20. *Annex 1: Approval of Methodology*, OFGAS 30 September 1994.

21. *The Domestic Gas Market*, House of Commons Trade and Industry Committee, 23-I, London, HMSO, November 1994.

22. *The Domestic Gas Market, Government Observations*, House of Commons Trade and Industry Committee, 29I, London, HMSO, November 1994.

23. For OFGAS the 4.19p is probably an embarrassment which it may try to eliminate even though it originally set it. Its defence against cross-subsidy is based on the argument that the £15 alone adequately reflects site costs. It produces an ingenious argument based on *avoidable* or marginal cost which can be largely ignored as government policy is that 'customers should pay the *full* cost [or *accounting* cost which includes their proportionate share of overhead] of the energy resources they consume.' On the basis of accounting cost the allocation to domestic site charges of about £270 million looks far too small compared to TransCo's own estimate for total customer costs in 1993 of £670 million.

24. *Gas Bill, Parliamentary Debates*, Hansard, 13/3/ 1995.

25. The Trade and Industry Committee, First Report - The Domestic Gas Industry, HMSO, 23-I, 23/11/95.

26. For example from: Dan Corry, David Souter, Michael Waterson, *Regulating our Utilities*, IPPR, 1994: 'So what should regulation be about? The simplistic answer put about by non-thinkers on the Right, is that the pursuit of the maximum amount of competitiveness is the only objective. (See for instance Colin Robinson of the Institute of Economic Affairs: "I would like to see all of [the regulators] promote competition to such an extent that their Offices wither away." *But who will regulate the regulators,* Adam Smith Institute, 1993)'.

27. There is a twist here to the issue of competition, monopoly and board remuneration. Why should a management receive high returns for running a profitable monopoly, particularly if it ran it under very different conditions of risk and reward when it was a nationalised industry? In fact BG was privatised nearly nine years ago and all the executive members of the board have changed since then. A management might have a vested interest in the riskier world of competition as justifying to it higher remuneration.

28. OFGAS' main concern seems to be to promote new entry into the domestic market. The task of the incumbent appears to be to make a 'phased withdrawal'. Therefore, even though there may be legislative provision for a levy to share costs, it may not be operated while any one firm is 'dominant' - technically this could mean an above 25 per cent market share. The incumbent can probably expect little protection against 'cherry-picking' - indeed this is regarded as the natural route of new entry. The only protection is rebalancing prices to reflect costs.

THE FUTURE OF REGULATION
OF THE ELECTRICITY SECTOR
RICHARD TURNER[1]

Introduction

This paper reviews the regulation of the UK electricity supply industry (ESI) since privatisation and considers what form economic regulation might take in the future. Economic regulation is defined as intervention by an external body in an industry to determine prices and or investment decisions. The discussion focuses upon the Generation business (the production of electricity) and the Distribution business (the transportation of electricity from the National Grid to consumers) as these are responsible for the bulk of the costs to consumers. I have attempted to describe and analyse these issues in a manner accessible to non economists and non specialists in the ESI. This inevitably requires simplifying a very complex picture which will not satisfy all readers and for that I apologise.

Key Issues in the Regulation of Electric Utilities

The need for regulation arises in a competitive market for two main reasons: firstly, because it is believed that the market is unable to deal with social and long terms strategic issues; and secondly, the market has barriers to entry which prevent economic rents (monopoly profits) from being competed away. Regulation is required where the activity is a natural monopoly[2] because the market is not a feasible mechanism for controlling behaviour.

In general economic regulation of electricity has three principle objectives: secure national strategic objectives, such as diversity of sources of supply and support for the coal industry; the continuing provision and development of the utility services; and, to prevent utilities from extracting long run monopoly profits and or operating inefficiently.

Although the principle objectives of regulation can be simply described, in practice any regulatory system has to balance different sets of interests. These are the interests of the stakeholders in the system. The stakeholders are consumers, shareholders, and the government. Each stakeholder has a different set of primary interests. Consumers are principally interested in low prices and security of supply, shareholders are interested in stability and adequacy of returns, the government is interested in economic efficiency, and depending upon it political complexion, equity. Some of these interests are in direct conflict and thus a judgement must be made as to the appropriate balance. A good regulatory system succeeds in balancing these different interests despite the inevitable conflicts.

The rest of this paper seeks at assess: how effectively the regulatory framework for electricity industry has balanced these interests; the extent to which there are pressures for change; and the direction that such change might take.

Background

The Electricity sector is unique amongst privatised industries in that it was restructured before flotation. The industry benefited from the experience of privatisation of British Telecom and Gas both of which were privatised as monopolies. It was recognised that if the ESI was to avoid the regulatory problems of a national monopoly then there needed to be a structural rather than a 'conduct' solution. This was first expounded in 1982 by Nigel Lawson and was formalised in the 1988 White Paper, 'Privatising Electricity'. The six principles articulated in the white paper were

● *Decisions about the supply of electricity should be driven by the needs of customers.*

● *Competition is the best guarantee of the customers interests.*

● *Regulation should be designed to promote competition, oversee prices and protect the customers' interests in areas where natural monopoly will remain.*

● *Security and safety of supply must be maintained.*

● *Customers should be given new rights not just safeguards.*

● *All who work in the industry should be offered a direct stake in their future, new career opportunities and the freedom to manage their commercial affairs without interference from government.*

The restructuring originally involved a break-up of the Central Electricity Generating Board (CEGB) into two generating companies, National Power and Powergen, and the National Grid (to become the National Grid Company (NGC)). The then Regional Electricity Boards were spun off to become separate PLCs each of whom retained a share of the NGC. National Power was intended to be big enough to absorb the problems of Nuclear Power.

The privatisation of Nuclear Power under the umbrella of National Power proved unworkable due to the misgivings of the financial institutions unwilling to accept the unquantified risks associated with Nuclear Power and thus Nuclear Electric was created. The outcome of this process was that National Power was privatised with over 50 per cent of capacity, Powergen with about 30 per cent with Nuclear Electric retaining the remainder. Thus what was left at the end of the restructuring process was an oligopoly in Generation.

A different industry structure was not adopted because the Governments overriding objective was to complete the sale of the electricity industry during the lifetime of the Parliament. This would not have been achieved if a new industry structure had to be created. The urge to privatise was driven by a political imperative: 'if we don't do it now we probably won't get another chance'. Few commentators expected another Conservative government to be elected at the next election.

The importance of the resultant oligopoly was the power it gave National Power and Powergen to set the prices in the spot market, known as the POOL. This arose not only as a result of their share of generation capacity but because they owned most of the marginal plant which effectively determines the market price. Thus the structural solution for the Generation industry failed to create a competitive market.

The Role of Competition

The strategy adopted for achieving the competition objectives laid out in the White Paper was one based on gradual transition to competition which was expected to last a decade. This strategy had a number of components:

● the coal industry was to be allowed to contract slowly with fixed price contracts for the period 1990-1993;

● post-1993 the Generators were no longer burdened by government obligations to support coal and could optimise fuel purchasing;

● the Regional Electricity Companies (RECs) were permitted to enter the generation market subject to a limit of about 15 per cent of their demand, or regional load;

● the supply market was to be exposed to competition in stages, initially with respect to I MW customers and subsequently other categories of customers up to 1998 when the market was to be fully liberalised;

● electricity prices were to be allowed to rise to reflect the, then estimates, of the full current cost replacement value of the assets, thus encouraging new entrants.

Much of this has happened, if somewhat more slowly than was anticipated. However, this strategy has failed to address the fundamental problem of the lack of real competition in the generation market stemming from the structure of the industry that emerged from privatisation.

The industry structure and proposed strategy to introduce competition that the incoming regulator inherited has placed him in an invidious position. The issue he faced was how to introduce competition in the Generation industry while at the same time satisfying pressure from consumers for low prices and from the government for support for the coal industry. In attempting to balance these interests the regulator has made a series of interventions to promote investment and control prices.

Interventions in the Generating Market

Economic Purchasing Review

The first such intervention was under the guise of the 1993 review of the REC economic purchasing obligation for the 'cost pass through' tariff market. Under this obligation *"RECs are obliged to purchase electricity at the best effective price reasonably obtainable..."* (Source: prospectus) and then pass that cost directly through to the customers. That this obligation was fulfilled was of particular concern in relation to the non-competitive, almost entirely small customer, franchise market where each REC has a monopoly.

The review took place against the backdrop of significant investment by the RECs in their own generation capacity. This plant was typically gas fired combined cycle gas turbines which were project financed with very small amounts of equity, and with loans guaranteed against a 15-year power purchase agreement (contract for difference).[3]

The costs of these agreements were passed on directly to the franchise customers. Thus effectively the RECs diversification into power generation was a risk free investment.

The review concluded that the contracts were 'economic' in that they compared well with alternative sources at the time, which were essentially coal contracts. However when evaluated against a different set of criteria based on risk, the contracts were significantly less attractive because the strike price of the contract was indexed to reflect changes in the major determinants of POOL prices such as fuel prices.

In many ways the review was an exercise seeking to provide an answer that legitimised the 'dash for gas' and supported the competitive strategy envisaged at privatisation. However while these Independent Power Plants (IPPs) led to an increase in capacity available it did not increase the amount of competition in the generation industry because the IPPs were financed in such a way that they had to run all the time in order to meet their financial obligations and thus were essentially price takers in the market. As noted above prices are set by marginal plant.

POOL Price Cap and Plant Disposal

In April 1994 OFFER (the Office of the Electricity Regulator) sought to apply both price restraint to the spot market for electricity and to force National Power and Powergen to dispose of 6000 MW of capacity. This move was in direct response to political pressure over rising POOL prices and an awareness that even with the expansion of IPPs the market was not effectively contested. OFFER felt that if agreement could be obtained then this would be preferable to an MMC inquiry. Under the agreement prices were to be capped for two years at 2.4 pence per kWh time-weighted and 2.55 pence per kWh demand-weighted (indexed to the RPI) and plant would be sold at a reasonable price.

This announcement exposed many of the problems with the structure of the generation industry. Firstly, the regulator had tacitly conceded, what commentators had always recognised, that the two principal players had unwarranted amount of market power. Secondly, that competition had not effectively been increased by the development of the IPPs as these plants were not bidding at the margin.

OFFER's intervention appears to have created as many problems as it was intended to solve. Firstly, new gas fired plant requires a demand weighted price of about 2.5-2.7 pence per kWh in order to be viable and thus the price cap effectively means that new plant is at best marginal. Secondly, the price cap has created uncertainty about whether it will be possible to ever remove the price controls.

At the time of writing, OFFER have yet to persuade the generators to dispose of the required plant. The principal problem is agreeing a price to scrap some of the excess plant. Most of the plant is old coal plant which is effectively written off and in practice has a limited life span. Nevertheless it has value to the generators. Its value to National Power and Powergen as marginal plant is extremely high because it will contribute to setting the price at any time. A company with a portfolio of plant, able to optimise dispatch, will benefit from this. However its value to an investor without a portfolio of plant, typically a new entrant, is principally as base load plant (a facility that always supplies power regardless of the bid price for the power supplied): a purchaser entering the market is likely to be able to purchase cheap imported coal and thus the 'marginal' coal plant will become base load plant. Such new entry will not, in any case, help to increase competition in the key areas of the merit order (where the cheapest power producer is commissioned to run first in consideration of the variable bid price for power supplied).

Regulation of Generation in the Future

The problems of the generating industry lay in the industry structure that emerged from the initial restructuring process. The original vision at privatisation of a competitive generation industry was compromised by the wish to dispose of nuclear generation as well as thermal and hydro generation capacity. The attempts to subsequently introduce competition have been compromised by consumer pressure for low prices and embarrassment at the profitability of the generating companies.

It is difficult to see how, without some serious attempt to alter the structure of the generation industry, either by breaking up National Power and Powergen or by restricting their ability to invest in new plant, the generation business can become a truly contested market.

Thus in the absence of fundamental change imposed by the regulator or government in the structure of the market it is likely we will face annual POOL price inquiries and *ad hoc* interventions for the foreseeable future.

Regulation of the Generation market will thus continue in some form or other. The effectiveness and efficiency of this intervention is unpredictable and likely to be driven by stakeholders interests. This will yet further increase the uncertainty in the industry and is likely to raise the cost of capital facing the Generators.

Regulation of the Monopoly Distribution Businesses

Distribution businesses are natural monopolies. Thus regulation in some form or other, either explicit or implicit will always be with us. At the time of privatisation the ideology of price cap regulation held sway. In essence the principles were that by setting a predictable rate of change of the price cap over the regulatory period those who could achieve efficiency gains more quickly than this rate of price change implied could retain them for shareholders. At the end of the regulatory period it was assumed that all the players would be brought back to level zero and a new price cap imposed that reflected the new cost structure. It was elegant and simple. Consumers would benefit over time from lower prices and from the incentives provided for companies to increase efficiency and make money for their shareholders. The approach to regulation would mirror a market in which economic rent would be competed away by new entrants.

However, what has become clear is that while price cap regulation may go some way to satisfying economic efficiency objectives it is not able to satisfy equally important objectives of transparency and equity. The vitriol currently expressed in the press and elsewhere about the share prices and wealth of the utilities is a failure of monopoly regulation to meet these objectives.

Perhaps the principal problem with price cap regulation is that it implicitly assumes that the regulator is able to identify the real current and prospective position of the company with respect to operating costs and capital expenditure and prospective efficiency gains. As has transpired, this is more difficult than any commentators at the time of privatisation thought possible. It is illuminating to consider the expectations at flotation of the performance of the RECs and the actual outcome.

The Initial Setting of the Price Cap

Market expectations at flotation were that the Distribution companies would achieve modest efficiency improvements. This expectation was based on the precedents of British Telecom and British Gas which had managed to achieve very little efficiency gains since they were privatised. In addition the RECs had put forward very high investment projections based on forecast load growth. The combination of low expected efficiency gains and high investment expenditure lead to relatively generous efficiency factors in the price cap which averaged +1.15 per cent.

The overall outcome of this price control was expected to lead to falling dividend cover and there was a perception that the RECs would be seen as low growth stocks valued primarily on dividend yield. These expectations were reinforced by comments at the time by analysts such as John Wilson of UBS:

> "compared to other regulated utilities the electricity industry and particularly the regional electricity companies are high risk"

and

> "Governments desire to maximise proceeds has led to extremely low dividend cover ratios; ... this exacerbates downside risk"

In fact the RECs have been a high growth stock, outperforming the market by up to a factor of three with dividends rising at 12 per cent per annum in real terms. As a wider indicator of performance the rate of return on capital employed in the RECs ranged between 29 per cent and 47 per cent compared with an national industry average of about 20 per cent. Thus it appears that low risk regulated utilities (technically with a Beta less than 1) have yielded returns that are more comparable to those one might expect from a high risk, leading edge technology company. The overall outcome of this situation is that now all but two of the RECs are debt free and two have negative gearing of about 20 per cent.

Thus the outcome has diverged dramatically from what was expected. In retrospect this can be seen to be due to two principle factors: firstly, the forecasts of capital expenditure was significantly higher than the outturn, due to the recession depressing new load growth and costs of capital expenditure being lower than anticipated; and secondly, the positive growth in prices combined with modest efficiency gains (OFFER estimate that "only 6 RECs expect controllable costs to have been reduced by more than 5 per cent in total between 1990 and 1995") had significantly increased operating profits.

The Distribution Review

Against this backdrop of an industry outperforming the original price cap OFFER undertook the Distribution price review which commenced in mid 1993 and produced a determination in August 1994. This review concluded that there should be a one off price cut of between 11 per cent and 17 per cent and an X factor of -2 per cent. The results from this review have been widely viewed as too lax. This is reflected in the analysts comments at the time:

> *"Share holders can only rejoice and behold the dividend growth laid before them by OFFER's largesse"*
> (Hoare Govett)

and

> *"The favourable Distribution review ... the regulatory regime is investor friendly"*
> (BZW).

As a consequence of the terms of the review and such comments as above the share price jumped by about 35 per cent from mid-July to the end of August to a level that exceeded the previous peak at the beginning of 1994. The subsequent bid by Trafalgar House for Northern Electric and their defence strategy merely brought to the public gaze a widespread view that the future price controls were too generous. The bad publicity over directors' salaries and share options added icing to the cake.

The outcome of this process is a widespread belief that the regulatory process has been discredited and that only fundamental change will restore credibility. It is apparent that this view has currency both within the Industry, Westminster, and public opinion as articulated by pressure groups and the media. It is appropriate to consider whether these views are merely reacting to an unfortunate combination of singular events or whether there is a real basis for concern.

In seeking to evaluate this issue it is useful to briefly describe the background to the Distribution review and the review process itself. Prior to the review OFFER had carried out just two previous reviews: that of the Supply business and that of Transmission. During the course of these reviews it appears that trust broke down between the two parties. The RECs felt that OFFER were not prepared to negotiate and OFFER believed that the RECs were not providing all the information that was necessary for OFFER to reach an optimum decision. Thus going into the review battle lines appear to have been drawn.

The process of the review required the companies to furnish the regulator with a great deal of information on historical costs, revenues, and forecasts for the same variables over the next regulatory period. Even though this information was checked and verified by consultants the process inevitably provided many opportunities for presenting a particular interpretation of reality.

Moreover, it appears that the review was not undertaken in a spirit of co-operation and intellectual honesty but rather a contest of wills and debate. It seems clear that the RECs saw the objective of the process to maximise shareholder value almost at all costs while the regulator appeared to wilt under the pressure and barrage of argument and counter-information. The outcome was a determination which, though proposing a one-off price cut averaging 14 per cent and an RPI-2 per cent price cap over the period, was widely seen to be lax, leaving too much of the surplus profits with the companies.

Key Constraints in a Regulatory Process

It is useful to try and identify the key constraints that the regulatory process faces to try and understand this outcome and assess its implications. Perhaps the most important constraint is that of asymmetry of access to information. This simply means that the companies know more about their business than the regulator ever can. This asymmetry leads to the possibility of disinformation i.e. the companies don't tell the regulator the truth or perhaps more accurately only tell part of the truth. This is known as adverse selection. The implication is that the regulator is kept in the dark and this increases the uncertainty surrounding his decisions.

The second element of asymmetry is changing behaviour after commitments have been made. This situation arises in the context of forecasts. For example, suppose I forecast reductions in my operating costs of 1 per cent while knowing that I can achieve 4 per cent. This is a particular problem in the area of capital expenditure where the relationship between expenditure and any output indicators suffers from a considerable time lag. However, it can also apply to forecasts of operating costs. Companies may be able to achieve efficiency gains at a more rapid pace than forecast.

In addition to asymmetry of information there is asymmetry of resources between the regulator and the companies. Thus in effect it is very much 'David against Goliath'. It is clear that the resources devoted by OFFER to the review were not sufficient to produce a robust outcome.

A further and perhaps most important constraint on the regulatory process is its requirement to set prices for a five year period. Forecasting is a hazardous process. Most forecasters would limit plausible forecasts to a two year time frame. To many, three years is beyond the foreseeable future. The fragility of forecasts is evidenced by reference to the original price formula at flotation which were based on expected load growth and increasing investment. Within two years the economy was in the worst recession since the Second World War and such growth did not take place.

Combined, these problems produce a situation where a high degree of uncertainty is likely to surround any determination. This may lead to determinations which are initially too lax, or too tight, or may become so over the period.

The Implications for Regulation

Does this degree of uncertainly matter? Some believe that it does not, because as long as consumers are seeing prices decline in real terms they are better off. Companies take the risks of delivering the price cuts, thus they should reap the rewards. That they are able to achieve these price cuts is a measure of the success of privatisation and the regulatory process. Moreover it doesn't matter from an economic efficiency perspective whether shareholders or customers get the benefits of increased efficiency as long as they are available to the economy.

This point of view implicitly assumes that economic efficiency is the only objective of regulation and that the issues of equity are unimportant. Moreover it assumes that the companies are achieving efficiency gains as rapidly as is possible. This is demonstrably not the case. Throughout the 1970s and 1980s the Distribution companies managed, on average, to achieve about 2 per cent efficiency gains per annum. It is not unreasonable to presume that these gains should have continued. Thus, even ignoring the benefits from privatisation one would have expected efficiency to have increased by 10 per cent over the period. Indeed this is reflected in the determination made by OFFER. As noted above the RECs do not appear to have achieved such gains.

However while the criteria of efficiency may be important, it appears to be a necessary but not sufficient criteria for a successful regulatory framework. Equity appears to have emerged as a key to most of the other desired attributes. If the criteria of equity is not satisfied then it appears that the system cannot be stable. The current debate is fundamentally not about efficiency or privatisation but that of equity. The political and public constituencies appear to demand that a different balance be struck between shareholders and customers. Thus if we are achieve the objectives of the different constituencies, i.e. financibility, stability, equity etc then a different approach will need to be taken to ensure that there appears to be sharing of the risk and rewards.

Thus it is likely that the structure of regulation of the RECs and other natural monopolies will change within the foreseeable future to one based on some form of profit-sharing arrangement. Such an arrangement would allow companies to recover normal costs associated with the business i.e. capital expenditure, operating costs, and costs of capital (subject to an efficiency constraint) but would require that any economic rent would be shared with the consumer.

This approach does not solve all the problems identified above however it does seek to mitigate the issue of information asymmetry and will go some way to satisfying the equity concerns that have emerged. This approach is being actively considered to apply to the San Diego Gas and Electric Company in California and is gaining widespread support elsewhere.

Notes

1. London Economics. The views and opinions expressed in this paper are mine alone and I take responsibility for any errors and misunderstanding.

2. An industry where economics of scale are such that one firm can produce at lower average costs than could be achieved by more than one firm in the industry.

3. A contract for difference is a financial instrument which fixes the purchase price of electricity into the future (Strike Price). It is called a contract for difference because all electricity must be bought and sold in the POOL thus payment is made by either party to a contract to compensate for differences between the POOL price and the strike price.

INDUSTRY STRUCTURE AND REGULATION
IN THE RAILWAYS SECTOR
IAN JONES[1]

Introduction

Despite recent controversy on the issues of senior executive pay and company profitability, there remains a strong underlying consensus that the UK's privatised utilities are here to stay in much their present form. Debate on the future of the utilities sector accordingly focuses on matters such as the development of competition (how quickly should competition be introduced and what obligations should be placed on new entrants?); on the form of regulation (is there a case for modifying the price cap approach?); on the specific duties of the regulator (should industry regulators have any locus on issues of executive remuneration and other aspects of internal company policy?); and on the organisation of the regulatory function (should there be a single 'super-regulator'?).

Railways clearly do not neatly fit into this pattern. There is no political consensus on the role of the private sector in the industry, and the Labour Party is committed to bringing the railways back under public control and possibly public ownership. There also continues to be vigorous debate on the technical and economic merits of the approach to industry restructuring adopted by the Major administration, and even on whether it will prove to be workable.

This lack of consensus on an appropriate structure and constitution for the UK rail sector justifies the approach followed in the present paper, which examines both structural options and the role of the regulator under different industry structures.[2]

Regulatory Roles in the Re-structured Railway Industry

The Railways Act 1993 provides the framework for the most wide-ranging and ambitious programme of industry re-structuring and privatisation yet pursued by the present Conservative administration and its predecessor. The principal features of the new structure were described in a White Paper, entitled 'New Opportunities for the Railways', published in July 1992.

The White Paper indicated that British Rail's existing track and signalling assets would be vested in a new organisation, to be known as Railtrack, which would be responsible not only for operating and maintaining the infrastructure, but also for train control and timetabling. Although Railtrack would remain initially in the public sector, the White Paper expressed the hope that it would be privatised, and in the event, this process has been accelerated, with a planned flotation date set for early 1996.

Railtrack would sell train paths to passenger service franchisees for the provision of passenger services specified in franchise agreements, and to open access operators, who would include the privatised successors to BR's existing rail freight businesses and operators wishing to provide passenger services additional to those specified in franchise agreements, possibly in competition with incumbent franchisees. British Rail's passenger rolling stock and the related traction equipment would be vested in a number of rolling stock companies (ROSCOs), who would in turn lease the equipment to the franchised train operating companies (TOCs). The revenue streams of both Railtrack (largely) and the ROSCOs (entirely) would be secured through contracts with the TOCs. Other elements of the re-structuring involve the 'spinning off' of BR's existing infrastructure and heavy maintenance operations into a number of separate businesses. The short-term commercial futures of these units would be secured through contracts with Railtrack, in the case of the infrastructure service businesses (ISCOs), and with the TOCs, in the case of the vehicle maintenance activities.

Instead of providing British Rail with a Public Service Obligation (PSO) deficit grant, subsidy will be mainly injected into the re-structured industry via the passenger service franchising mechanism to be run by a new public sector agency, the Office of Passenger Rail Franchising (OPRAF). Freight services will continue to be eligible for subsidy if the subsidy secures worthwhile congestion relief and environmental benefits.

Like the re-structuring itself, the regulatory regime established in the 1993 Act is both complex and distinctive in several respects, compared to arrangements elsewhere in the UK privatised utilities. Responsibilities for economic regulation are divided between two agencies. The Office of the Rail Regulation (ORR), is responsible for regulating the interface between Railtrack and the train operators, for whom Railtrack is a monopoly supplier of infrastructure services. ORR is also responsible, concurrently with the Office of Fair Trading (OFT) for ensuring fair competition between train operators. Responsibility for protecting the interests of consumers with respect to the conduct of the TOCs is vested in OPRAF, and will be exercised through the terms of the franchise agreements, which will specify minimum service levels, and may also specify maximum fare levels in situations where the TOC would enjoy significant market power. It is likely that the franchise contracts will also contain financial incentive mechanisms to encourage effective delivery of franchised services.

The role and responsibilities of ORR are also distinctive in several respects. First, the regulator's duties, set out in Section 4 of the 1993 Act, are unusually complex. The list of duties contained in Section 4(1) is familiar enough from previous legislation; protecting the interests of rail service users; promoting economy, efficiency and competition in the provision of rail services; promoting through ticketing, enabling travellers to buy a single ticket for services provided by more than one TOC; and enabling railway businesses to plan for the future development of the business with "a reasonable degree of assurance". The real novelty occurs in the provisions of Section 4(5), which require the regulator to take account of any guidance given to him by the Secretary of State for an initial period until 31 December 1996, and also to "have regard to the financial position of the Franchising Director in discharging his functions".

The requirement to take account of ministerial guidance is unique in UK privatisation legislation, and has been criticised as putting at risk the independence of the regulator, which has been regarded as a fundamental feature of previous legislation. On the other hand, not to have done so, in a situation where the legislation left important aspects of industry conduct and financial performance subject to regulatory determination, might have introduced an even higher degree of risk into a financially fragile industry. This enhanced 'regulatory risk' might, in turn, have impeded still further the transfer of railway businesses into the private sector.

This distinctive form of regulatory risk stems from another highly novel feature of the 1993 Act, which ceded significant influence to ORR over the financial outcomes in the new structure. This influence is exercised through the provisions in Sections 17 to 22 of the Act, which require the regulator to approve all track access agreements. The track access agreements are in many ways at the heart of the new industry structure. They will on the one hand determine Railtrack's income, and hence its value at flotation, through the level of charges set and the duration of the contracts. They will also affect the level of subsidy required to secure the output of franchised rail services, both directly through the level of track access charges, and indirectly through the structure of track access charge contained in the contracts and through the on-rail competition they will allow. Hence the requirement for the regulator to have regard to the position of the Franchising Director in making his determinations.

A final distinctive feature of the regulatory provisions in the 1993 Act is that ORR is given a substantial role alongside the Franchising Director in the highly complex set of procedures covering service closures set out in sections 37 to 50 of the Act.

ORR has formally exercised its powers under the 1993 Act since 1 April 1994. During this period the rail regulator, Mr. John Swift QC, has been active in issuing a series of consultation papers on key areas of regulatory policy, including track access charges, on-rail competition, and the provision of through ticketing.[3] Following the consultation process, the regulator has subsequently issued policy statements on the level and structure of track access charges and on the development of on-rail competition.

Before reviewing these documents and the dilemmas they expose, it is helpful to set the scene by examining some alternative approaches to industry re-structuring to the one contained in the 1992 White Paper.

Alternative Structural Models

The 1992 White Paper emphasised the importance of increasing the competitive pressures on the supply of rail services both to drive down the cost of provision and to improve service to customers. Overseas experience of railway restructuring indicates that competition can, in fact, be introduced into the supply of passenger (and freight) services in several different ways. What may be referred to as the 'open access' approach seeks to encourage on-rail competition, through the separation of train operation from the ownership and operation of infrastructure assets. Separation of infrastructure and train ownership and operation is regarded as necessary because of the difficulties observed in other network industries, such as telecommunications and gas, in ensuring fair competition in the final market between a vertically integrated owner of an essential facility and 'independent' service providers. This broad approach has been followed in Sweden and also in Germany.

In addition to the separation of infrastructure and train operation, other features of the open access approach are as follows:

- Access to the rail infrastructure would be controlled through contracts between the infrastructure owner and the train operating companies. These contracts would specify the rights and obligations of each party. Charges might either be negotiated or be based on a published tariff.

- The charges paid by train operating companies to use infrastructure would be based on the costs (primarily of wear and tear on track and structures and electric traction current) which varied directly with the use of the system. In the more heavily used or congested parts of the network, these 'basis' fees might be supplemented by charges reflecting congestion costs (somewhat analogous to road pricing charges proposed for London and other major cities) or the costs of expanding the capacity of the system. In Sweden, the track access charges regime is intended to mirror that applied to road vehicles; accordingly, train operators also pay the equivalent of a vehicle excise duty at a fixed rate per vehicle.

- Given the technical characteristics of rail infrastructure, the revenues thus raised would fall short of the full costs of providing the infrastructure. The infrastructure owner would receive a deficit grant from government and would remain as a public sector agency. In Sweden, the infrastructure owner, Banverket, has been established as a government agency equivalent to the National Highways Authority, and like the Highways Authority, does not receive access fees, which are paid to the government.

- Given a charging system of this kind, there would be a core of profitable passenger and freight services which could, in theory, be provided by privatised train operating companies. In theory, as in the civil aviation sector, or in the markets for local bus services in the UK, competition, or the threat of it, would act to secure the interests of consumers.

- Rail services for which fare revenues fell short of train operating costs and infrastructure charges would be provided through a franchising mechanism.

● The traction equipment and rolling stock might be owned either by the train operators, or by equipment leasing companies, or, as in the civil aviation sector, by a combination of the two.

An alternative approach would be to retain the traditional vertically integrated character of railway operations, but to introduce competition for the market, through a process of franchising vertically integrated railway operations. This approach has been followed in Argentina, for example, in some suburban rail operations in the USA, and, interestingly, in the Channel Tunnel Rail Link (CTRL) project.

The vertically integrated franchise model would be applied by dividing the rail network geographically, by line of route, and the franchisees would take over all aspects of rail operation in that sector. Other features of this approach include the following:

● Franchises would be awarded through a competitive bidding process, in which the franchise would be awarded to the bidder offering to provide pre-specified services for the minimum level of subsidy. Bidders would be subject to pre-qualification 'tests' for financial soundness, technical competence etc.

● Franchise contracts would generally be limited to specifying minimum levels of service. However, in sections of the network where the customer base was substantially captive, franchise contracts would also specify the maximum fares to be charged, and the quality of service, in terms of punctuality, overcrowding etc to be provided, in order fully to protect the interests of users.

● The length of the franchise contract would vary according to the weight placed on various policy objectives. Competitive pressures would be maximised by relatively short term franchises. However, longer term franchises would encourage franchises to be more innovative (since they would enjoy the benefits of innovation over a more extended period) and would be necessary if franchisees were to be encouraged to undertake significant investment in new rolling stock or infrastructure assets. Passenger service franchisees would be able to sell track access rights to rail freight operators.

● Franchises might or might not be offered on an exclusive basis. However, even if they were not, this approach is unlikely to support anything other than very indirect forms of competition, between franchisees, for example in the case where services between major centres were available on different lines of routes.

Each approach has distinctive virtues and drawbacks. Under the open access approach, commercial train service output is 'market driven', given the price of the infrastructure services purchased by train operators. This approach also addresses directly some of the problems of competition between road and rail, if road use is indeed underpriced. It permits effective competition between train operating companies to develop if demand is sufficiently intensive. Although the infrastructure authority would remain in the public sector, there is no reason, in principle, why it should not be obliged to contract out many of its activities, such as track maintenance, allowing competitive pressures to be brought to bear on costs at all stages of the value chain.

The vertically integrated franchise approach scores highly in encouraging the cost efficient provision of subsidised passenger rail services through the periodic franchise process. By retaining a vertically integrated structure, it largely avoids the deadweight cost burden of dealing with interdependencies via contract mechanisms. By bringing a relatively high proportion of value added under the direct control of the franchisees, it ensures that competitive pressures are felt throughout the value chain. Finally, by restricting the scope of on-rail competition, this approach allows any surpluses above the directly variable costs of infrastructure to be reflected in franchise bids, hence reducing the level of subsidy compared to the open access approach.

Regulatory Issues in the Re-structured Railway

The industry structure now being implemented under the provisions of the 1993 Act represents an uneasy amalgam of the two structural models discussed in the next section. British Rail's activities have been vertically separated into an infrastructure owner and a set of train operators, ostensibly to promote on-rail competition through an open access regime. At the same time passenger services are to be franchised, and franchisees will pay track access charges which, together with whatever revenue is contributed by freight operators, will allow Railtrack to recover the full costs of operating and replacing its assets.

A major problem for the rail regulator is that this hybrid approach to restructuring creates a strong tension between the objectives of promoting on-rail competition and containing subsidy through the franchising mechanism. As the regulator's consultative document on competition recognised, the stronger the threat of competition from open access services, the more negative will be the franchise bids. This conflict was also recognised in the initial guidance given by the Secretary of State to the regulator in March 1994, which talked of the need to "moderate competition" to ensure the successful launch of the first generation of franchises.

The consultative document discussed several possible approaches to moderating competition, including modifications to the access charging regime. The policy statement has opted for an administrative approach, which will limit Railtrack's ability to make 'open access' train paths available if they would materially affect the incumbent franchisee's revenues. The measures mean that there will be little, if any, open-access competition until April 1999; although restrictions will be relaxed somewhat in the following three years, they will still constitute a substantial barrier to entry.

The other key area for regulatory decision under the new structure concerns the level and structure of charges to be recovered in track access charges for franchised passenger services. Here, ministerial guidance recommended the regulator to adopt essentially the regime established as the basis for Railtrack's vesting. This would allow Railtrack to set charges which, after 2-3 years would recover its operating expenses, plus a set of depreciation charges derived from the cost of modern equivalent assets (MEAs) needed to meet the expected future level of demand, plus an 8 per cent real rate of return on the depreciated value of the assets.

The regulator's policy statement on the level of charges has significantly modified the initial regime, arguing that revenues should be rebased to a level some 8 per cent lower in real terms than those set for 1994/5, and that charges should fall by 2 per cent per annum in real terms in each of the following five financial years. In reaching this decision, which is said to be fully compatible with Railtrack's continuing financial viability, the regulator appears to have judged that the opportunities available to Railtrack for cost reduction and revenue enhancement are greater than originally anticipated. He has also indicated that Railtrack should be run as a "single till business", so that the revenue gains from exploiting its property portfolio should be shared with TOCs. Finally, he has indicated that the company's cost of capital as a private sector business would be less than 8 per cent.

On charging structures, the regulator has taken a more cautious line in recommending the approach followed in initial contracts, in which only a very small proportion (around 10 per cent) of the total charge faced by franchisees is directly variable with franchisee output. An important implication of this approach is that open access operators would have been able to purchase spare train paths at very low cost to compete with incumbent franchisees. In the absence of the administrative restrictions referred to earlier, such a regime would have encouraged the emergence of widespread open-access competition in the more densely used parts of the network, and could have significantly depressed franchise bids.

Future developments

Future students of public administration in the UK will find much
to interest them in the development of public policy in respect of
railway privatisation. Above all, they will wish to understand the
reasons why such a relatively complex approach has been followed
in a financially fragile industry. Compared, for example, to a scheme
based on franchising a set of vertically integrated line-of-route units,
the government's preferred approach has involved possibly very
significant additional up-front costs of reorganising the industry, and
creating a web of contractual mechanisms to replace internal
command relationships. Yet the main potential benefit of this
approach, in the form of the emergence or threat of on-rail
competition as a discipline or incumbent suppliers, has been denied
in order to limit subsidy. This can reasonably be described as an
outcome involving much pain for little gain.

Nevertheless, the extra costs are largely sunk, and there will
inevitably be strong pressures to retain something close to the
existing structure, especially if Railtrack flotation proceeds as
planned, and if the first round of franchising is completed. In this
event, many elements of the regulatory regime have been settled by
the regulator's policy statements on track access charges and on-rail
competition; they would need to be revisited only if ministerial
guidance on the weights to be attached to different duties was
significant revised.

ORR will face important decisions in the next several years on how
much consolidation of franchise operations along lines of route to
accept. Greater consolidation would reduce pressure on OPRAF's
franchising budget by restricting still further the scope for on-rail
competition and by allowing operators to integrate service provision
and ticketing arrangements. Another area in which the regulator will
almost certainly be active involves the track access contracts
between Railtrack and rail freight companies, who operate under an
open access regime and must negotiate charges with Railtrack. In
this area, the regulator's primary responsibilities are to ensure that
access charges are both reasonable in terms of level and non-

discriminatory as between different operators. The non-discrimination requirement stems from the provisions of EU Regulation 91/440, which sets out conditions for open access to rail networks. Although the regulator has issued a short policy statement indicating his general approach to the issues, it is clear that its detailed application will be keenly contested by Railtrack and its rail freight customers.

In the longer term, especially if pressures on the franchising budget were relaxed, there would be a case for developing approaches to regulate the level of on-rail competition through pricing mechanisms. One approach, which was not examined in the regulator's consultation document, would be to develop the charging structure so that train operators paid additional charges for train paths in certain heavily used or congested sections of the network. Such a development would have the advantages of encouraging the efficient use of capacity in an open access environment and of being non-discriminatory as between different operators.

If the rail industry structure set out in the 1997 White Paper is revisited, however, ORR's future would be very uncertain. If industry structure moved towards the vertical franchise model, for example, industry conduct would be regulated largely through franchise contracts, and there would appear to be no role for ORR. The Swedish approach would produce a structure with strong affinities to arrangements in the stage carriage bus industry in Great Britain following the Transport Act, 1985. By analogy, on-rail competition, or the threat of it, would restrain the conduct of service providers, and any competition policy issues could be addressed through the Competition or Fair Trading Acts, and, once again, the case for a separate industry regulator might be difficult to establish.

Notes

1. Ian Jones is Director of National Economic Research Associates.

2. Other discussions of the rail issue in IPPR publications are found in the Waterson chapter of *Regulating Our Utilities* (Corry, Souter, Waterson IPPR 1994), and in *New Economy*, Spring 1995, in particular, 'Hitting the Rail Buffers' by Bill Bradshaw.

3. The regulator is able to influence the availability of through ticketing by specifying obligations in the licenses which are granted to TOCs.

Some IPPR Publications

Regulating Our Utilities
Dan Corry, David Souter & Michael Waterson
Sept 1994 ISBN 1 872452 94 9 £9.95

Too much discussion of regulation either dwells on the minutiae or simply attacks some of its less agreeable outcomes. the papers in this report focus on the purposes of regulation and best means of delivering them. Competition, although a vital component of any strategy, must be seen as a tool and not an objective of regulation. The three papers in this book have a new approach to regulation that puts the national interest first.

New Economy
A journal for new thinking on economic policy

Whether a professional economist, or a non-specialist who wants to know about the latest thinking on the centre-left, *New Economy* is indispensable reading. This quarterly journal, produced by the IPPR and edited by Dan Corry, covers all aspects of economic policy in a lively and refreshing way. Contributors include leading economists from the universities, the City and business.

For a sample copy and subscription information write to *Marketing Department, Dryden Press, 24-28 Oval Road, London, NW1.*

Reshaping the German Social Market
David Goodhart
April 1994 ISBN 1872452 84 1 £7.50

Once the most dynamic economy in Europe, Germany now has a per capita income roughly the same as Italy's and a public sector debt problem as bad as Britain's. However, the author argues that the German model will continue to deliver better economic and social outcomes than the liberal market economies of Britain and the US.